The Basic Essentials of

ALPINE SKIING

by Carol Poster

Illustrations by

Lucie Lavallee

ICS BOOKS, Inc.
Merrillville, Indiana

THE BASIC ESSENTIALS OF ALPINE SKIING

10 9 8 7 6 5 4 3 2 1

Printed in U.S.A.

All ICS titles are printed on 50% recycled paper from pre-consumer waste. All sheets are processed without using acid.

ACKNOWLEDGEMENTS

The cover shows two skiers enjoying Naskiska in British Columbia. Illustrations in this book were drawn from photos of local skier Janet Nelson at Mt. Bachelor, Oregon.

I would like to thank Steve Howe, and the rest of the staff at the Sports Guide, for advice and support during the writing of many of the articles that eventually, in much altered form, coalesced into this book. Similar thanks are due to the editors and staff of Network, The New Press, Ski Magazine, and Women's Sports and Fitness.

Published by:
ICS Books, Inc.
1370 E. 86th
Merrillville, IN 46410
800-541-7323

Library of Congress Cataloging-in-Publication Data

Poster, Carol.
The basic essentials of Alpine skiing / by Carol Poster
p. cm. — (The Basic essentials series)
Includes index.
ISBN 0-934802-40-8 : $5.99
1. Skis and skiing. I. Title. II. Series.
GV854.P576 1993
796.93—dc20 93-29016
CIP

TABLE OF CONTENTS

1. Physical Conditioning 1
2. Alpine Ski Equipment 5
3. The Anatomy of a Ski Resort 15
4. Ski Schools and Lessons 27
5. Your First Lesson 33
6. Beginning Technique 43
7. Intermediate Technique 49
8. Advanced Technique 55
Appendix 59
Glossary 65
Index 68

1. PHYSICAL CONDITIONING

It's often said that you don't ski to get in shape but you get in shape to ski. Although you certainly don't need to be a world-class athlete to enjoy cruising the smooth, well-groomed slopes of most modern ski resorts, investing a few hours a week in a preseason conditioning program will enable you to put in longer and more enjoyable hours on skis than if you did nothing to prepare other than an occasional twelve-ounce curl while watching Warren Miller ski films.

Skiing puts unusual demands on your body because of the conditions under which it occurs. You ski in cold weather, at high altitude, wearing heavy awkward gear, and perform movements unlike those of any other sport. As a new skier, you'll often find yourself working harder and using more muscles than an expert. Skiing is a skill sport. As you develop your technique, you'll glide effortlessly down steep slopes at high speeds, letting your skis and gravity do the work for you, but your first runs down an easy hill may have you sweating despite an outside temperature in the low teens.

Adapting to Altitude

Think about a picture of Colorado with soaring snow-capped mountains and a crystal clear deep blue sky. The same environmental conditions that make the average ski area so breathtakingly beautiful also make it literally hard to breathe. Many western resorts have a base elevation of over seven thousand feet and summits over ten thousand feet. Most of the population of the United States, outside the intermountain west, lives quite close to sea level.

If you live near sea level, it usually takes two or three days to acclimatize to the high altitude and dry air of most ski resorts. There are, however, several strategies that can help your body adapt to altitude more quickly and comfortably.

Relative humidity at many western resorts often averages under 10 percent.

Skiing in cold weather can cause you to become severely dehydrated without feeling thirsty. Often, if you feel tired for no apparent reason, the cause is dehydration. To prevent this, drink at least eight or ten glasses of water each day.

Dry air affects the outside of your body as much as the inside. Frequent—but easily preventable—problems include chapped lips and skin. Petroleum jelly (ideally with SPF 15 sunblock) will protect your lips. Apply body lotion or moisturizer to your entire body in the morning, before bed, and after washing your hands during the day. Save money by investing in a large container of inexpensive lotion—cheap brands are just as effective as more expensive ones.

You've probably heard warnings about how the thinning ozone layer has made sunscreen essential for outdoor activities. At high altitude, there's less air between you and the sun than there is at sea level. (That's why the sky is such a beautiful deep blue—less moisture to scatter the light). Combine thin air with light amplified by reflecting off snow, and the result is exposed skin the color of boiled lobster and puffy swollen eyes, unless you take measures to protect yourself.

Start by selecting a good pair of sunglasses or goggles. An amber or Serengeti tint will help you distinguish contours in flat light—when a slight overcast eliminates the shadows that help you judge the terrain. Apply waterproof sunblock (SPF 15 and over) on all exposed areas of skin, being careful not to miss the lobes of your ears (in case they don't quite stay covered by your hat) and the underside of your neck and chin (to cope with reflected light). If your nose drips, reapply sunscreen every time you blow it. Once or twice a day, at bathroom stops, lunch, or on chair lifts, reapply sunscreen thoroughly.

Once you've finished caring for the outside of your body, you need to think about nutrition. Be sure to eat adequate protein (to help your body manufacture more blood cells for transporting oxygen) and complex carbohydrates (for energy).

If you do consume alcohol after skiing, remember that the effect of alcohol increases with altitude. One beer at a resort is the equivalent of two at sea level. Also, since alcohol has a dehydrating effect, try to consume an extra glass of water for each drink.

Conditioning Your Heart and Muscles

Skiing demands a combination of cardiovascular endurance, muscular endurance, and strength. Any aerobic exercise—including running, fast walking, biking, swimming, roller blades, cross-country skiing, or aerobic dance—performed for at least thirty to fifty minutes three or four times a week, for at least six to eight weeks, will prepare your heart and lungs for skiing. The primary muscles you'll need to strengthen are your quadriceps, with some work on your abdominals (upper, lower, and obliques) and the other major muscle groups in your legs and buttocks as well.

Probably the most ski-specific off-season exercise readily accessible to the average person is bicycling. It uses many of the same muscles as skiing. Alternate long, steady rides with short bursts of energy (hills or speed) to simulate a variety of ski terrain. On a stationary bicycle vary resistance for the same effect. In-line skates (rollerblades) also work ski-specific muscles and skills.

If you work out at a health club, you can use a variety of machines for pre-ski conditioning. Alpine ski simulators are ideal, but rowing machines, stair climbers, Nordic ski simulators, and inclined treadmills also work ski-specific muscles. For the abdominal muscles, after your aerobic workout try a few sets of situps—bend your knees, lift half way up, and add a twist at the top to tone your obliques.

For aerobic dance enthusiasts, many studios close to ski areas offer pre-ski conditioning classes. Otherwise, try step aerobics for a good all-round low-impact workout that works many ski muscles. If you like dance and want the best possible training for leg strength, flexibility, and balance, and are willing to commit to a long-term program, consider ballet. You'll need to spend a year in beginner classes before you'll become sufficiently skilled in the basic movements to get a real workout, but if you plan to tackle advanced ski slopes (very steep or mogulled), ballet is ideal preparation. Not only will it improve your explosive strength, range of motion, and coordination but toe shoes are the only footwear sufficiently uncomfortable to prepare you for a day skiing in badly fitting rental boots.

The Skier with Special Needs

Although skiing can be a physically demanding sport, that doesn't mean that it's inaccessible to the disabled. Most resorts will help locate sighted guides for blind skiers; outrigger poles are available for the one-legged skier; and sleds open up most mountains to those who cannot manage regular skis. Neither weight nor age is a barrier to skiing. For Colorado "over-the-hill" ski club members, ski life begins after sixty.

If you have chronic knee injuries, consult your orthopedist before skiing. Although many advanced skiers return to the sport—and even Olympic competition—after serious knee injuries, the carving movements involved in advanced skiing actually place less stress on the knee than the twisting and skidding movements involved in beginning skiing. Your orthopedist can design a conditioning program and recommend a protective brace for your knees.

2. ALPINE SKI EQUIPMENT

Alpine skiing is a gear-intensive sport. This doesn't necessarily mean expensive (see the appendix), but skiers do need to plan their equipment more carefully than participants in many other sports. While runners can manage with a good pair of shoes, a T-shirt, and shorts, skiers may need hats, gloves, parkas, pants, long underwear, gaiters, skis, boots, poles, glasses or goggles, fog cloth, sunscreen, and lip balm. Luckily, for new skiers, you can use a combination of items already in your wardrobe and rental equipment to avoid investing extensively in the sport until you're sure it's worth a permanent commitment.

Ski Specific Gear

There are four things you need for skiing that you probably won't find lying around your house: boots, skis, bindings, and poles. For your first few ski lessons, you'll want to rent this equipment—the soft boots and short skis best for learners don't perform well for advanced skiers, and the long skis and stiff boots favored by experts are dangerous as well as uncomfortable for new skiers.

Boots

Ski boots are your most important piece of equipment. They are constructed in two parts—a hard plastic outer shell for control and a softer fabric-covered liner for comfort and insulation. Your boots transfer the motion of your feet and legs to the skis as efficiently as possible; racers and expert skiers place serious performance demands on their boots at the expense of comfort. Beginners or infrequent skiers demand maximum comfort. Professionals, such as ski instructors and patrol, and frequent recreational skiers balance comfort and performance.

Alpine ski boots are composed of heavy stiff plastics, weigh a few pounds each, and bend your ankle forward at an angle that makes stairs a major hazard. When you first try on ski boots, they all seem awkward and uncomfortable, but by the end of ski season, you won't even notice them.

Typical boot designs include rear entry, overlap closure, and composite. Options include custom fit and built-in or attached heaters. The main trade off, just as in other expensive pieces of equipment like cars or computers, is adjustability versus ease of use. A basic rear-entry ski boot with one buckle and a minimal number of adjustments takes only a few seconds to enter or remove, but will generally not have the performance characteristics necessary for extreme speeds or terrain. An advanced (racer or expert) boot design with hundreds of knobs, screws, buckles, and microadjustments will give superb performance for an expert skier, but is often a waste of time and money for an intermediate who might only ski a few days a year.

For your first few days skiing, it's best to rent a "beginner package"—skis, boots, and poles—either from a store at the ski area or in your home town. Renting at the resort is probably a better idea—so you can go in and exchange equipment over lunch if something isn't working. Arrive at the rental shop early and pick up your gear. Ski boots are designed to be worn with one relatively thin pair of wool socks (smooth, not ridged). Make sure you have no wrinkles in your socks, and slip on the boots. Adjust the buckles to hold your legs and feet solidly in place without cutting off your circulation—don't be embarrassed to ask the rental attendant for help if something doesn't feel right. Spend five to ten minutes walking around the shop in your ski boots—staying on the carpet to avoid wearing down the boot soles. If anything hurts, talk to the staff and get it fixed. Remember, if your feet are moderately uncomfortable after five minutes in the store, they'll be excruciatingly painful after five hours on the mountain.

If, after a few days, you decide that you like skiing enough so that investing in your own gear makes sense, the first piece of equipment you'll want to buy is boots. Try renting several different models—and if you find a boot you like, buy it. Remember, there is some variability in manufacturing, and a new pair of boots won't fit just like a worn pair of rental boots. If you can't find a pair of rental boots you like, start talking to your ski instructors, friends, and people with whom you share chair lifts for recommendations. Go to a magazine rack in a sports store, book store, or supermarket or head to your local library to find the annual gear reviews in the ski magazines until you've located a few potential boot choices.

Whether you decide to buy a boot model you've tried or not, spend at least fifteen to twenty minutes walking around the shop in the specific pair you intend to buy and have a technician fix any problems you encounter. Off-the-shelf insoles and arch supports, longer bails to accommodate large calves, custom footbeds or foam can give you a perfect fit. Don't settle for less.

Tips for People with Cold Feet: Boots are designed for precise fit with a single pair of socks. *Don't* wear extra socks for warmth. The extra bulk will decrease the blood circulation in your feet and actually make them feel colder. If you do have problems with cold feet, the easiest solution is to wear a warmer *hat*. When you lose heat from your head, your body senses that it's getting cold and decreases blood circulation to the extremities (hands and feet) to conserve heat—so, essentially, if you don't wear a hat, your feet and hands will feel cold.

If you're dressed warmly and your feet still feel cold, you can either buy boots with built-in battery-operated heaters or add on heaters to your existing boots. A less-costly alternative is neoprene overboots—an especially good idea if you plan to ski in very cold climates (Wyoming, Montana, Canadian Rockies, New England).

Alpine Skis

Although most Alpine skis look identical, except for the brightly colored cosmetic design on the top, actually they vary considerably in design and performance characteristics. A downhill racing ski, designed for skiing almost straight downhill at very high speeds, is quite different from a powder ski designed to make short turns in soft snow.

Although modern skis are constructed of complicated layers of metal, plastic, and other high tech materials, functionally they haven't changed much since the prehistoric skis that have been found by Scandinavian archaeologists.

The most important part of a ski is the bottom because it is the part that comes in contact with the snow. The bottom of an Alpine ski is composed of three parts: two metal edges and the "base," a large, flat area of P-tex (a special type of plastic). P-tex is close to frictionless, so when you place a ski flat on the snow it will slide downhill quickly and smoothly. When, on the other hand, you want to change directions or stop, you control your motion by digging the sharp metal edges of your skis into the snow.

The sides (technically, sidewalls) and top of a ski are somewhat less important. Their main functions are to shed snow, to protect the stuff inside, and to sell skis. Ski cosmetics (the pretty designs on the topskins) change yearly and can cause skiers concerned with style to indulge in frequent buying sprees to stay up to date. Less fashionable skiers then buy the slightly used (recycled!) pairs on sale for less than half their original cost, and feel morally superior.

The core, or inside of the ski, contains materials that help determine the ski's performance characteristics in various complex and unpredictable ways of interest only to engineers and advertisement writers—as a skier, you'll find that two or three minutes on the hill will tell you more about a ski than an entire book filled with technical specifications and laboratory tests.

Ski Performance Characteristics The main characteristics that affect how a ski will perform on the snow are length, sidecut, stiffness, and width.

Length. Longer skis are faster and more stable at high speeds. They're also harder to turn and heavier. Beginners usually start on short skis (150 cm.). Advanced recreational skiers choose skis from 180 to 207 cm., and downhill racers and speed skiers use skis from 210 to 240 cm.

Sidecut. Sidecut is the curvature of the ski's sides. Generally, the shovel (front) and tail (back) of Alpine skis are wider than the waist ski (center). A ski with a deep sidecut will make smaller radius (tighter and quicker) turns than one with little or no sidecut. For best performance at very high speeds (over fifty mph), downhill racers and speed skiers use skis with minimal sidecut.

Stiffness. Torsional stiffness (resistance to twisting) helps skis grip the snow in turns. Lengthwise stiffness (resistance to bending the tip toward the tail) affects performance in several ways. Soft skis turn and skid easily and are very comfortable for new skiers, but they tend not to perform well for the high speeds and the precise maneuvers of expert skiing.

Width. Wider skis are more stable than narrow ones, but narrow skis are more responsive and turn more easily.

Although there is a significant gap between beginner and expert gear in many sports, the differences in performance characteristics are far more drastic in skiing. A new cyclist may not need a $1500 mountain bike—but she could still ride one; $150 running shoes might be overkill for your first jog around the block, but they'd still be usable. However, a new skier simply would not be able to control a pair of 200 cm. slalom racing skis.

Most skiers learn on short skis and progress very quickly to longer skis. A five-foot-six-inch female skier might start skiing for the first time on 150 cm. skis, move to 160s the second day, 170s the third day, 180 or 185s for a few weeks, and by the end of the season settle on 195s as a comfortable length.

Since it's hard to learn on long, stiff skis, and the short, soft beginner skis you use for learning won't perform most expert maneuvers, it doesn't really make sense to buy skis until you've skied at least ten to fifteen days and are no longer outgrowing your equipment every few days. Rental skis are widely available. Hold off on investing in skis until you're consistently making parallel turns on groomed runs and occasionally venturing onto advanced terrain.

Bindings

Bindings do three things: hold your skis and boots together while you ski, release your boots from your skis if you fall, and prevent your skis from flying away down the mountain after they've released. Bindings are a critical factor in ski safety—the advances in contemporary bindings design have made the stereotypical skiing accident, the broken leg, extremely rare.

When you first rent skis, the technician at the rental shop will adjust your bindings for you. She'll ask you to fill out a chart indicating your skiing ability, height, and weight; then she'll adjust the bindings on both skis to fit your boots. Next, she'll adjust the release setting, depending on the information you supplied to her. *Don't lie!* Expert skiers, who need to stay in their skis while traversing irregular terrain at high speeds, require very high release settings so they won't come out of their skis while executing difficult maneuvers like landing on steep slopes after jumping off a cornice. New skiers, however, often fall at low speeds, and their bindings should release easily to prevent possible injuries.

As well as attaching your boots to your skis and releasing to prevent injuries, your bindings also prevent your skis from taking off and flying downhill after they release. You'll notice two plastic-covered metal prongs called ski brakes, one projecting down from each side of the binding, which retract out of the way when your boot is placed in the binding. When your binding releases in a fall, the ski brakes dig into the snow so they'll stay somewhere near you in case of a fall, rather than taking off, achieving a terminal velocity of over one hundred miles per hour, and impaling a few dozen skiers on their way into the trees.

Tips for Rental Ski Safety When renting skis, check the white plastic friction plates that go under the boot toe. If they're damaged (pieces missing), ask the technician for a different set of skis. If you have chronic knee problems, make sure that all bindings you use release upward at the toe (protects ACL). Also, intermediate skiers and above might consider using a lower release setting (by 1/2 or 1 on DIN scale) on their injured leg.

Poles

In Alpine skiing, you use poles primarily to time your turns—you lightly reach downhill and plant your pole (tap the snow with it) to initiate a turn. Far less elegant, but equally common, uses of Alpine poles include pushing yourself through flat areas, picking up dropped gloves, delicately moving small fallen skiers (referred to as "anklebiters") out of your way, and scratching the skis of people who cut in front of you on lift lines.

To try on poles, turn a pair upside down. Place the plastic handle ("grip") on the floor, hold your arms by your sides, and grasp the poles just under the baskets. If your forearms are parallel to the floor, the poles are the right length.

Two safety considerations are important in selecting poles. The top of the grip should be larger than your eye sockets to prevent your losing an eye in a fall (this eliminates cut-down Nordic poles). The second is that breakaway straps, which pull out of the pole under stress, can prevent shoulder sprains in falls when your pole sticks in the snow and you fly downhill, or when you're skiing through trees and your poles catch on a branch.

Other Gear

Winter Clothes

Ski clothes must cope with cold, wind, and moisture in a sport that alternates five- to thirty-minute periods of intense activity (skiing) with ten- to twenty-minute periods of sitting still on chair lifts exposed to wind and cold. The easiest way to insure you'll never ski again is to dress in a cotton turtleneck, a few warm sweaters, parka, long johns, and jeans. Jeans will get wet—then freeze. Your warmest sweaters and parkas will cause you to sweat—and then your wet cotton turtle neck will leach heat from your body as you shiver on the chair lift contemplating pushing your best friend off the chair after she asks you if you're having fun.

While only an extremely avaricious salesperson would claim you need ski-specific clothes like a $750 powder suit in order to be a happy skier, you do need to invest in some technical outdoor sports gear to ski comfortably. The most important parts of your ski wardrobe are a wicking long-sleeved top, ski gloves, and a pair of thin wool socks. The rest can be rented or improvised.

The best way to dress for skiing is by wearing several light layers of clothing, which can be adjusted easily for rapidly changing mountain weather, rather than a few heavy layers. These layers need to serve the following three functions:

Wicking—Drawing moisture (sweat) away from your body.

Insulating—Retaining body heat.

Weatherproofing—Protecting the inner layer from rain, snow, and wind.

Wicking Layer Your wicking layer normally consists of two pieces, a top and bottom, both made of "wicking" fabrics designed to transport moisture away from the body. The ideal top is a zip turtleneck. For bottoms try long johns or tights (lycra or other wicking fabrics). Make sure seams either are flat or can be pulled up above the tops of your ski boots. Because you press your shins forward into your boots while skiing, a ridge (big seam, wrinkled sock) between the front of your shin and your ski boot can cause uncomfortable bruises.

Special tip for women: Choose a sports bra in lycra or a wicking material for skiing. Motion control isn't an issue, but cotton fabric gets clammy and metal hardware or scratchy nylon can chafe.

Insulating Layer The best insulating layers stay warm when wet—polyester pile (fleece) or wool are common choices. For tops, fleece jackets or wool sweaters from your current wardrobe are perfectly adequate. Fleece pants or extra layers of warm underwear work well until you get committed enough to the sport to invest in a good pair of ski pants. Although fashions change from year to year, the most functional bottom layer is stretch wool pants in a bib style (so they don't gap in the back and let in cold air) that go over your boots (and keep the snow out). Dark colors (black or navy) will need cleaning only once a season.

Weatherproofing Layer For a weatherproofing layer, waterproof breathable fabrics (e.g., Gortex, H2NO) are ideal, but nylon, especially when treated with water-repellant spray will handle most ski conditions. The level of protection you'll need depends on the weather. In fairly mild weather or light snow, a nylon jacket and pile or wool pants will be adequate; in rain or heavy snow (either wet snow or high volume snow), you'll probably need waterproof breathable tops and bottoms. Avoid nonbreathable waterproof jackets—they may protect you from snow, but you'll end up drenched with sweat.

Gloves

Heavily insulated leather or combined fabric and leather gloves are an absolute necessity. Your hands are exposed to cold weather, wind, and snow while you ski, and thin street gloves simply won't help.

Select gloves that are constructed to conform to the shape of your hand to minimize awkwardness. If you're very sensitive to cold, try wearing thin liners of silk or wicking fabrics for extra warmth. Liners will also protect your hands when you (inevitably) need to take off a glove on the chair lift in order to rummage through your hip pack to find and use tissues or sunscreen or lip balm. Mittens are even warmer than gloves, but many skiers find them clumsy. Overmitts—nylon mittens that go over gloves—combined with liners will keep your fingers comfortable to well below the temperatures at which any sane person skis. Gloves with removable linings work well throughout the season.

Socks

Ski boots should be worn with one thin pair of socks. They should leave room to wiggle your toes but hold the rest of your foot firmly in place. If there is extra room in your boots, either try a smaller size or fill the excess volume with off-the-shelf or custom inserts (insoles, arch supports, heel lifts, footbeds). Using extra socks to fill the boots ruins the boots' performance. Make sure that your boots aren't so tight as to impede your circulation and make your feet feel cold.

Traditional ski socks are made of wool, sometimes blended with silk, polypro, or nylon. Some brands have extra thick fabric covering the area in front of your shin, a feature of benefit especially to mogul skiers.

When you put on ski socks, make sure to smooth out all wrinkles to prevent bruises.

Head and Neck

You can lose a tremendous amount of heat from your head unless it's properly covered. For warm-weather skiing (over 35 degrees), a fleece headband covering your ears and keeping your hair out of your face may suffice, but for colder weather you'll need more substantial protection.

Just as you cover your body with wicking, insulating, and weatherproofing layers, so too do you need to layer your head gear. The ideal inner layer is a balaclava—basically, a one-piece stocking that covers your head and neck with a small opening for your eyes and nose—in a silk or synthetic wicking fabric. It's essential that this layer *not* itch. Over your balaclava goes the insulating layer—either a wool or fleece hat. Choose a hat with long flaps that cover your ears. Finally, the hood of your jacket makes a weatherproof layer. If your ears are particularly sensitive, wear a fleece headband under your balaclava.

To prevent warm air from sneaking out between your jacket and hat add a soft fleece "neck gaiter"—a one-piece scarf worn around your neck which can be pulled up over your nose during long, cold chair lift rides.

Eye Protection

You need to cover your eyes when you ski. The combination of bright sun, thin air, and reflected light from snow can easily cause "snow blindness"—painful swollen eyes, headaches, and temporarily impaired vision. Your eyes need protection from cold and wind as well as light.

Ordinary sunglasses will work for mild weather and infrequent skiing. Remember to use retention straps (e.g., Chums or Croakies) to keep glasses attached to your head.

More dedicated skiers invest in heavy-duty eye protection. Glacier glasses, with leather flaps that shield the sides of your eyes, work for skiing and other sports as well, as do shields and wraparound glasses. Ski goggles, with double lenses and foam covered vents, offer the best protection for your eyes while skiing and are also more resistant to fogging than glasses. Goggles are also required for racing—you don't want to rely on sunglasses if you hit a slalom pole at thirty mph.

A vision problem unique to winter sports is fog. When warm, moist air from your nose and eyes contacts the cold surface of your glasses it condenses into fog or ice, partially or completely obscuring your vision. Ski shops sell fog cloths impregnated with fog-resistant chemicals. Wiping your glasses or goggles with fog cloths before skiing and occasionally during the day usually helps. Heated goggles, with battery-powered fans, are probably the most effective solution.

While sunny weather can cause vision problems in the form of snow blindness, haze or snow can result in what is called "flat light." When the sun is obscured, you don't have shadows to help you read the terrain—so you won't recognize bumps and indentations in the snow until they throw you off balance and leave you lying in a heap at the bottom of the slope. Glasses or goggles with amber tints help your depth perception in flat light and snow.

Special Precautions: If you wear contact lenses, you'll need good glacier glasses or goggles to protect your eyes from the wind. If you wear glasses, you'll need prescription sunglasses or goggles you can wear over your glasses. The goggles-over-glasses combination is extremely fog prone—either consider prescription goggles or heated goggles or be prepared to purchase fog cloths in bulk.

Small (but Necessary) Stuff

Skiing is definitely a gearhead's sport. While rich skiers who spend entire winters at Aspen or Sun Valley (referred to by locals as "the fur brigade") may blithely acquire every odd piece of gear invented by the ski industry, and hardy ski bums create the majority of their equipment with duct tape, the majority of skiers prefer the middle ground—buying whatever is necessary for skiing comfort but forgoing the status symbols.

Hip packs were common among skiers for several years before they became fashionable and started appearing in exotic materials in expensive boutiques. A cheap nylon version works perfectly well.

The reason for carrying gear in a hip pack is to avoid the necessity of rummaging in your pockets while dangling one hundred feet above the ground on a wet slippery chair lift in a high wind. Rotate your hip pack around to the front of your body before you get on the lift, and your gear will be easily accessible.

Some possible ski accessories you might want to carry with you are:

Facial tissue: Your nose will drip when you ski. If you're sufficiently crass (or have a Nordic ski background) you'll solve this problem by wearing gloves with soft absorbent backs; otherwise, carry tissues. (Some resorts provide these at the base of chair lifts, but bringing your own is a better idea. This also will prove useful in heavily used and poorly maintained restrooms.)

Sunblock: Carry a small tube of waterproof sunblock inside a plastic sandwich bag so that when the lid comes off (it will), the rest of your gear will still be safe.

Lip balm. Invest in a brand with sunscreen (SPF 15 or over). Stick versions tend to harden in cold weather and melt in hot weather. The tubes of lip jelly handle temperature variations best.

Neoprene face mask: These small, inexpensive gadgets are a necessity for very cold (under 10 degrees) weather skiing.

Fog cloth. Always carry two in case you drop one.

Powder cords. Long cords that lead you to your skis after a fall are very useful if you're skiing deep powder (over six inches)—they can save you hours of digging for lost skis in ungroomed snow. If you ski primarily groomed runs (beginner and intermediate), you won't need them.

CAUTIONARY NOTE: Don't put your wallet, car keys, or anything expensive or hard to replace in a hip pack or a pocket containing anything you might need on a chair lift—unless you want to spend the rest of your ski day hunting through several feet of snow for whatever you've dropped from the lift. (Just after spring thaw, many impoverished ski bums go hiking under chair lifts and collect an astonishing quantity of gloves, ski poles, goggles, and miscellaneous junk dropped by unwary skiers.)

Putting it all Together

For typical western ski weather—18-35 degrees, sunny, moderate wind—you might wear a polypro turtleneck, lycra tights, fleece pullover or warm sweater, polypro long johns, Gortex shell, wool ski pants, wool socks, neck gaiter, silk balaclava, wool hat, sunglasses, and lined Gortex gloves and carry a hip pack containing waterproof sunblock (SPF 15), lip jelly, Kleenex, and fog cloth. If the weather cools down, pull the neck gaiter over your head and close the hood of your jacket. If you get too warm, remove the neck gaiter and unzip your jacket.

For extremely cold weather (under 20 degrees, high winds), add an extra layer of thermal underwear and a second hat. Wear mittens or overmitts on top of your gloves. Protect your face with goggles and a neoprene face mask.

In warmer weather, eliminate the insulating layer, and just wear an unlined shell over your wicking layer. For summer skiing (over 60 degrees), a long-sleeved wicking turtleneck and lycra tights are perfect. Remove linings from adjustable gloves or try bike gloves or light-weight cross-country ski gloves to keep your hands sweat-free and protected. No matter how inviting the weather, don't strip to shorts and a T-shirt. Not only is opaque clothing far more effective than sunblock, but you also want your skin protected in case of a fall. Snow partially melts in warm weather and then refreezes overnight into a jagged mass that some skiers call "cheese grater ice." You don't want any skin exposed while sliding down refrozen snow after a fall at twenty or thirty mph.

The worst possible skiing weather is a full day of rain or heavy wet snow. Although most local skiers cope with these conditions by going home, diehards can protect themselves from even the worst weather—and enjoy uncrowded runs, lifts without lines, and fresh snow. Every time you ride uphill on a chair lift in wet weather, you end up sitting in a mixture of water and snow. The bottom part of a rubberized waterproof (NOT breathable) rain suit will protect your pants. A nylon poncho (belted at the waist) over a waterproof breathable jacklet will insure a full day of dry skiing in the worst weather.

For the indigent or unprepared, you can fashion your own rain suit from two heavy-duty lawn/leaf size garbage bags and duct tape. For pants, cut off the corners of one bag to make leg holes, step in, duct tape the "legs" to your pants, and then tape the top of the bag around your waist so it doesn't fall down. Create a top by cutting arm and neck holes in the bottom of your second bag, and create a custom fit with a duct tape belt. Although this outfit might get you some odd looks from the tourists at expensive resorts like Aspen or Deer Valley, it's a standard trick among locals at powder havens like Alta.

3. THE ANATOMY OF A SKI RESORT

There are three major categories of ski resort: small local resorts, medium-sized resorts, and large destination resorts. Each type has its own advantages and shortcomings.

Small local resorts are inexpensive and friendly. Their ski schools often specialize in teaching new skiers. They're often family oriented and have close connections with local schools. Some offer women's ski programs that meet weekly for four or six weeks and serve the dual purpose of improving your skiing skills and introducing you to potential skiing partners of your own skiing ability. The main drawback to small resorts is lack of variety, vertical, and challenging terrain. Especially in the East or Midwest, you may be able to ski every single run in a small resort in a single hour, and the terrain is unlikely to challenge the expert skier. Small Western resorts, on the other hand, may lack the glamour and elaborate base facilities of their larger counterparts, but—in such cases as Utah's Brighton, Solitude, and Park West—will offer excellent skiing at moderate prices. For beginning skiers, small resorts are ideal. The terrain is unintimidating, you won't get in trouble if you get lost, and the price is right.

On the opposite end of the scale from the local resort is the popular-destination mega-resort like Vail, Mammoth, or Lake Louise. Lift tickets (and everything else) are expensive, but these mountains offer something for every skier from extreme steeps to challenge the hard-core adrenaline junkie to entire separate beginner mountains, and every imaginable type of terrain in between. You can spend days on these mountains without ever skiing the same run. For the advanced skier, or families with varying ability levels who plan vacations together, these resorts are ideal. For the beginner, however, it makes sense to learn at a smaller and less-expensive area and then try a bigger mountain when you're ready to ski all of it (usually after ten to twenty days of skiing).

Between the small local resorts and the popular mega-resorts are a variety of mountains ranging from substantial to moderate in size.

Some resorts, while providing a variety of terrain, are famous for certain special features. Experts, for example, challenge themselves at Utah's Alta, Wyoming's Jackson Hole, Colorado's Telluride, or Norquay in the Canadian Rockies. Powderhounds favor Grand Targhee (Wyoming), Powder Mountain (Utah), and Sunshine (British Columbia). For summer skiing try Bachelor (Oregon) or Blackcomb (British Columbia).

You'll have the best ski experience if you select a resort based on a realistic appraisal of your needs. If you're into a luxury vacation, with good food and shopping being as important as skiing, a Spartan expert mountain like Alta or a low-key mountain like Utah's Sundance might be disappointing—but you'd probably love Sun Valley (Idaho) or Colorado's Front Range. A quiet family group would enjoy Idaho's Schweitzer or Colorado's Purgatory more than the glitz and high prices of Aspen (Colorado) or the hectic pace of Hunter (New York).

On the Road to the Resort

The most difficult and dangerous part of a day skiing is the drive up to the resort. Many resorts are located at the top of long, steep winding mountain roads covered with snow and ice. The best way to cope with access to ski resorts is to use public transportation or (for destination skiers) to stay in walking distance of the resort. However, if you need to drive to and from ski resorts, there are several things you can do to make bad- weather driving considerably safer.

The ideal ski car has four-wheel drive and high clearance. Front-wheel drive is better than rear-wheel drive. A manual transmission works better than automatic, and power steering should be avoided (it decreases your ability to sense traction). Rear defoggers and rear windshield wipers are useful—and new wiper blades are a good idea. For ease in cold weather starts, use a lightweight motor oil.

The best tires for foul-weather driving are studded snows; mud/snow tires with exaggerated treads do a good job; all season tires will work on roads that have been well plowed—but won't provide enough traction for narrow mountain roads during major snow storms. If your car does not have four-wheel drive and good snow tires, you should carry chains in your car. In many states, the highway patrol requires four-wheel drive or chains for mountain driving during storms, and snow tires, chains, or four-wheel drive for any winter driving in mountains.

Two fifty-pound bags of salt, dirt, or kitty litter (college students can substitute empty beer cans and junk food wrappers) in back of your car will provide extra traction for your rear wheels. Scattering any of these substances behind your wheels will help you get out of parking spaces. Salt placed just under your tires before you leave for a day of skiing will melt enough snow to give you perfect traction when you exit your parking space at the end of the day.

Other useful pieces of equipment include an ice scraper and a long brush to clear snow and ice from a parked car. A traction shovel, designed so that you can place it under a car wheel and use it as a ramp, helps you get out of parking places or get back on the road after sliding off. You can spray chemical de-icers (under $5 per bottle) on your windshield if it starts to ice while you're driving. Chemical or battery-powered lock de-icers insure that you can get back into your car (carry them with you or leave them outside your car—a de-icer in the glove compartment of a locked car isn't very useful). Jumper cables are useful year round—and cold weather is harder on batteries than warmer weather.

If you're driving long distances through remote areas—roads that get less than one or two cars an hour—you should consider carrying survival equipment in your car to insure your safety in case of accidents or impassable roads. If you need to stop your car in winter and wait for plows or rescue, you should not run your car engine—to avoid problems with exhaust fumes and running out of gas. Instead, carry warm sleeping bags (one bag rated to +10 and a few blankets or a second bag will work for almost any weather you'll encounter). A few pounds of trail mix and granola make good emergency food. For water, melt snow with a camping stove or solid fuel pellets. A few long books and a flashlight can provide entertainment.

When you're driving on snow or ice, the most important rule is to drive gently. Go more slowly than normally, make gradual rather than abrupt turns and lane shifts, and change speeds (accelerating or slowing) gradually. To prevent accidents use the following protocols:

Always look ahead and anticipate all maneuvers so you have time to perform them gradually.

Slow your car by taking your foot off the gas and downshifting. Avoid braking when possible.

If you need to use your brakes, pump them gently. Hard braking usually causes your car to skid.

If you need to slow down for a curve or corner, slow down first, then turn. (Braking and turning at the same time causes skids).

Don't accelerate hard (this may cause your wheels to spin). Maintain momentum going up hills. If you're going too slowly, you'll lose traction.

If you feel your wheels starting to spin (turning very quickly but not gripping the road) shift UP one gear (e.g., from second to third).

Hold your steering wheel lightly, and don't overcorrect small slithers.

Drive defensively. Stay well back from cars in front of you (at least double the distance you would on dry roads), and check the cars behind you in your mirror. If you see another car starting to slide, do what is necessary to avoid its hitting you.

If your car starts to skid, turn the wheel into the skid until your wheels are pointed in the same direction as the car, and downshift. Wiggle your wheel very gently (less than 1/4 inch) until you feel resistance—which means that you have traction again—then steer out of the skid.

If you're not accustomed to driving in snow, find a deserted parking lot (suburban malls or supermarkets after the shops close are ideal) and practice skidding and recovering.

At the Base Area

If you've driven to a resort, you'll park and then walk or take a shuttle bus to a central area usually called a base or lodge. At small resorts a single small building may contain all the skier facilities including the equipment rental shop, lift ticket sales, lesson sales, cafeteria, and bathrooms. At larger resorts, these facilities may all exist at several different locations or be split among several different locations. If you're new to a resort and plan to rent equipment or take lessons, allow at least thirty minutes for finding the facilities you need.

In Alpine skiing, you only ski down the mountain. The resort provides mechanized uphill transport—for a fee. To get access to uphill transportation ("ski lifts"), you need to purchase lift "passes" or "tickets."

Most resorts offer a variety of pricing options for lift tickets. The most expensive ticket is the standard "all day adult" pass. (Sometimes resorts charge even more for access to a tram or gondola—usually worth the investment only for experts.) If you plan to ski for several days at the same resort, consider investing in a multiday pass. Youth and senior citizen discounts are widely available. Many resorts offer heavily discounted lesson/equipment/lift pass packages for beginners. Ski Industries of America has co-sponsored a free (gear, lesson, and pass) yearly "learn-to-ski" day at several resorts every January. Many resorts offer discounted passes early (November through mid-December) and late (March or April) season, and resorts near urban areas frequently discount weekday passes. It's also worth inquiring about corporate discounts and special prices offered through local supermarkets and sports stores or as part of travel packages. Frequent skiers usually invest in "season passes" good for unlimited skiing for an entire ski season. At most resorts, you can obtain free or very inexpensive season passes by working three to five days on pre-season trail maintenance or other chores in September or October.

Physically, most single-day lift passes are approximately index card size pieces of self-adhesive paper, sold stuck to waxed paper backing. You're given (or forced to locate on your own) a V-shaped bent wire to attach your pass to your ski pants. Slip the wire through the metal ring designed for that purpose on real ski pants or the hole of a zipper pull or a belt loop on regular pants. (Don't attach your pass to any garment you might take off if the weather changes). Fold the lift pass in half, then peel off the backing, and fold the pass in half around the wire with the sticky side facing in. Your pass should be worn where the lift attendant can see it easily.

Season or multiday passes are usually worn on a string around your neck. To avoid having a pass flapping in your face as you ski, remember either to tuck it inside your jacket before each run and pull it out as you approach the lift or use a safety pin to fasten the cord to your jacket just above the pass itself.

When you buy your pass, remember to ask for a "trail map" which shows the layout of the resort. If you plan to take lessons, ask whether you can buy them at the same place as the lift tickets. If not, get directions to where lesson tickets are sold (this may be in a building quite far from the main cashiers). When buying lesson tickets, make sure to ask where and when the lesson will meet—and how long it takes to get there.

Tip for the Indigent: Resort prices, due to the seasonal nature of the economy (ski area businesses must earn a year's income in a five-month ski season), tend to be very high. Shop in advance in a nearby city for supplies if you plan to stay at a resort. Just as Park City locals usually drive down to Salt Lake or Vail locals go into Denver for supplies, so you should consider shopping in cities on your way up to a ski condo. Day skiers should consider bringing rather than buying lunch.

Reading Your Trail Map

A trail map shows the location of the trails or "runs" on which you ski down the mountain, the lifts that take you up the mountain, and various other skier facilities like restaurants, rest rooms, ski school meeting areas, and parking lots.

Trails are marked according to a standard system nationwide. Green circles represent beginner terrain, blue squares represent intermediate terrain, and black diamonds are for advanced skiers. Some resorts also use double black diamonds or red and yellow triangles to indicate areas skiable only by experts in good snow conditions. Three major factors determine trail ratings: pitch, grooming, and obstacles.

The pitch, or steepness, of a run is a good measure of its difficulty—the steeper a run, the harder it is to control your speed and the further you'll slide in case of a fall.

Most resorts invest heavily in machines that compress and flatten the snow to make it more easily skiable. This process is called grooming. Beginning and intermediate skiers should stay on groomed runs, but advanced skiers enjoy the challenge of snow in its natural state.

The final determinant of the difficulty of a ski run is the presence of obstacles. It takes far more skill to negotiate a narrow trail through the woods than a broad open "highway," even if the two are similar in steepness and snow conditions. Narrow rock-lined "couloirs" or "chutes"—where a slight mistake can result in serious injuries—are the exclusive realm of experts.

Another factor that determines the difficulty of a ski run is snow conditions. The easiest snow for most skiers is "packed powder"—groomed, new, dry snow. "Corn"—soft melted and refrozen snow with a velvet texture—is fun for all skiers. A few inches of new ungroomed dry snow (powder) over a groomed base is similar to groomed snow, but deep ungroomed snow ("bottomless powder"), the ultimate ski experience for experts, is quite difficult for new skiers. (Even advanced skiers have problems when encountering powder for the first time). Two other unpopular types of snow are "ice" and "crud." Ice—snow that has melted and frozen solid—requires advanced skiing skills and well-maintained skis. A major problem with ice is that if you fall, you keep on sliding until the terrain levels out or you collide with a solid object like a lift tower, rock, or tree. Most skiers (other than professional ski racers) avoid steep runs in icy conditions. Another highly unpopular type of snow is ungroomed, new, heavy, wet snow, which skiers call by such names as "crud," "mashed potatoes," "wet cement," and "Sierra cement." It's almost impossible to turn your skis in this type of snow.

When you decide which runs to ski, take snow conditions into account. If you can barely ski black diamonds (advanced runs) in ideal conditions (corn or packed powder), you should stay on blues (intermediate runs) in ice or crud.

Although the trail rating system is theoretically standardized, there are significant variations from resort to resort. For example, some of the blue runs at Utah's Snowbird (a resort with outstanding expert ski terrain) are as difficult as many of the blacks at the neighboring Park City.

In addition to signs identifying trails, you'll see a few others at most areas. SLOW SKIING signs, placed in congested areas, should be self-explanatory. Small red or orange flags warn of obstacles like rocks or tree roots underneath the snow—try to ski fairly far away from these. Roped off areas—surrounded by ropes stretched between thin poles planted in the snow—are closed to skiers, as are all slopes signed CLOSED. Signs reading "EXPERT SKIERS ONLY," red and yellow triangles, and red squares marked "CLIFF AREA" are for experts only—if you aren't skiing black diamonds easily, don't even think about skiing these areas. Sometimes you'll see a slope roped off with entrances (gates) between the ropes—enter the slopes only at the gates—and be prepared for difficult terrain or bad snow conditions. Ropes or fences marked "SKI AREA BOUNDARY" mark the end of where the ski patrol run "sweeps" checking for injured skiers. "Out-of-area touring" should only be done by experienced skiers carrying avalanche rescue equipment after asking permission from the ski patrol.

Another feature you'll see on ski slopes is person-high poles (usually red or blue) planted in the snow at fifteen- to fifty-foot intervals. These "gates" are located on racecourses and they show racers where to turn as they go down the hill. If you accidentally stray onto a run set up as a racecourse, ski down the edge of the run as far away from the gates as possible to avoid being hit by a racer. Although "running gates" (skiing down racecourses) is fun, paying a few dollars to ski a recreational course (available at most areas) is preferable to sneaking into one where you don't belong and possibly getting injured or having your lift pass removed by the ski patrol.

The Ski Patrol

The ski patrol are resort employees whose job is to insure your safety. They start work long before the resort opens in the morning, checking for hazards on the mountain. Avalanches are a potential problem in many areas—the patrol are responsible for checking snow conditions on avalanche-prone slopes. If a skiable run or a slope above a ski run has built-up snow that is likely to slide, the patrol will try to trigger the avalanche before you start skiing. They shoot explosive charges at avalanche-prone slopes so that the shock waves from the explosions will cause any unstable snow to break loose when it can't hurt anyone.

Although modern equipment is now available for shooting down avalanches, up until the 1970s World War II army surplus mortars were the weapon of choice. In one incident legendary in the Utah ski community, an Alta avalanche crew accidentally shelled the Brighton parking lot.

If the crews can't cause potentially unstable snow to slide, they'll rope off the area so it's inaccessible to skiers. (This is one reason why you shouldn't duck ropes to get untracked snow—you might end up buried in it.) The patrol will also advise skiers interested in out-of-area touring of the avalanche forecast for the day—but they don't actually do avalanche control or rescues beyond the area boundary. This safety factor is one reason why even experts pay to ski resorts when they could cruise the rest of a mountain range for free (another reason is uphill transport).

During the ski day, members of the patrol ski around the area, assisting tired, lost, or injured skiers and enforcing safety regulations (warning or pulling passes of drunk or reckless skiers who are endangering others). You can recognize the ski patrol by the large white crosses on their jackets.

Finally, the patrol rescue injured skiers. Some members of the patrol may be certified EMTs, and most are certified in CPR. They provide downhill transport in the form of snowmobiles or toboggans to the resort medical facility where experts will examine your injuries and either treat them or perform first aid and recommend that you visit a physician. The quality of orthopedic care at resorts is often outstanding—for several years, one of the three top orthopedists (for knees) in Salt Lake City worked at Snowbird—skiing all day with a beeper and returning to the base area if called on to assist injured skiers.

At the end of the day, members of the patrol "sweep" the area, skiing every possible route down, looking for tired or injured skiers and assisting them down to the base area.

In Case of Emergencies

Contrary to popular opinion, ski injuries are quite rare—statistically, driving to a supermarket is more dangerous (and much less fun) than skiing—but when they do occur, resorts have quite elaborate rescue services in place.

Usually, injuries involve falling. As you lie on the snow, assess your injury. If nothing hurts very much, clean off your goggles or glasses, get up slowly, gather your equipment, and start skiing gently. If you notice any dizziness or lack of coordination, consider riding down the nearest lift or asking the ski patrol for help.

You will find that the overwhelming majority of skiers are quite generous about helping others. If you've just performed a "garage sale" wipeout, scattering your gear all over the slope, usually everyone heading in your general direction will pick up pieces of gear and bring them down to you. If you're seriously injured, they'll also notify lift operators to send the patrol to you, and often stay with you if you want company while waiting. As your skiing skills develop, you should also consider helping fallen skiers—like good driving manners, it's a matter of karma.

The most common ski injuries are sprained thumbs. These cause minor discomfort (ice and ibuprofen at night will help) but won't interfere with your skiing.

The most common serious injuries are knee and shoulder sprains and broken bones (legs or arms). Normally, these are very painful. DON'T try to ski away from them. Have someone help you remove your skis (if this can be done without exacerbating your injury) and place them tails down in the snow to form a vertical cross or X-shape just uphill of where you're lying. (This is an international symbol for injured skiers.) Ask passing skiers to summon the patrol. The easiest method to communicate with the patrol is to request that a lift attendant call them on the radio.

Uphill Transport

In order to ski down a hill, first you need to get up to the top. Some New Englanders claim the earliest mechanized uphill ski transport in North America was invented in Woodstock, Vermont, in 1934 when Clinton Gilbert attached a continuous length of rope to the rear wheel of a Model T Ford to haul skiers uphill. In the late 1930s and after (with a brief hiatus for World War II) Alpine ski resorts with mechanized uphill transport have spread across the country, enabling millions of skiers to experience the thrills of downhill cruising without the drudgery of uphill hiking.

Lift attendants stand near the loading area (bottom) of lifts to check passes and assist skiers getting on the lift, and also at the top of the lift to assist unloading (getting off the lift). All lifts are equipped with variable speeds and emergency stops so that the attendants can stop the lift in case of accidents or slow it for skiers who need a little extra time. Lift attendants also will send up dropped gear with the next skier—so you don't need to worry about getting in a chair lift and picking up a dropped pole or glove at the same time. Many types of lifts also function as downhill transport. If you find yourself tired after lunch or at the end of the day (these are the times when most ski accidents happen), rather than struggle to ski down the mountain, you can always request a ride downhill.

You enter most lifts through what is called a "maze"—a set of lines carefully constructed out of poles and ropes designed to direct skier traffic efficiently. The surface of the snow is usually slick and icy from heavy traffic, and there is a high concentration of people in the area—so unless you're a very strong skier, you should slow down before entering a maze and then slide forward gently, propelling yourself with your poles. (Maze lines usually aren't wide enough for skating.)

If the lift is designed for two or more skiers and you're skiing single (alone), as you approach the lift look for other unpartnered skiers. Extroverts usually shout "SINGLE!" and cruise outside the maze waiting for a single skier on line to raise a hand or pole. Shyer skiers politely ask individuals, "Are you single?" Since lift rides range from five to twenty minutes (duration is usually specified on your trail map), aim for a compatible partner (some life-long relationships and many weekend romances start on lifts).

When you're joining another single skier already in line, you can slide past other skiers in the maze or duck under ropes—apologizing profusely or explaining as you go. This is NOT permissible under any other circumstances.

There are four main types of uphill ski transport, or lift: surface lifts (T-bar, rope tow, platter); enclosed (trams and gondolas); chair lifts; and helicopters and snow-cats.

Surface Lifts

Surface lifts (sometimes called drag lifts) dominated the early history of Alpine skiing but have since been retained only for special uses—usually short stretches of relatively flat terrain.

The simplest type of surface lift is the rope tow. It consists of a continuous loop of rope that moves slowly around top and bottom terminals. To be pulled uphill, you hold both your poles in the hand away from the rope, step near the rope, with your skis parallel to one another approximately shoulder-width apart, and knees slightly bent. You grab the rope itself (or a metal handle if they are present). As long as you hold on, the rope will tow you uphill. If you get in trouble (drop a pole, cross the tips of your skis), let go of the rope, move quickly out of the way of the skiers coming up behind you, ski down to the bottom, and start again. If you fall, roll away from the rope to avoid causing pile-ups. If you see a fallen skier ahead of you, again, drop the rope and step off to the side. Do the same thing—dropping the rope and moving away from it—at the top of a rope tow (or at your destination, if it comes earlier) as you would to avoid obstacles.

Another single skier surface lift is generically called a platter. It consists of a metal plate (roughly the size of a Frisbee) attached to a metal bar hanging down from a moving overhead rope. You stand in the loading area with both poles in your outside hand (the one farthest away from the platters) and wait for a platter to swing by with your legs spread slightly apart and your feet parallel. You grab the metal pole above the platter (or the lift attendant hands it to you), pull the platter through your legs so that the plate rests behind your buttocks, close your legs, gripping the pole slightly with your thighs, and let the platter tow you uphill. As you reach the top of the lift, pull down on the pole so the platter is a few inches behind your hips, spread your legs slightly, pull the platter out from between your legs, release it gently, and glide away from the lift. (Males should perform all these actions very carefully.)

The third major type of surface lift is the T-bar. It consists of an inverted T-shaped bar hanging down from a moving overhead rope. It is designed to be ridden by two people of approximately the same height simultaneously (unless you're an experienced T-bar rider DON'T share one with a person more than six inches shorter or taller than yourself). Just after one bar passes, you and your partner step in a loading area and wait for the next one, standing with your skis parallel and slightly separated and your poles held in your outside hand (the one farthest away from the other skier). Look back over your inside shoulder. As the bar approaches, both skiers reach back for the bar, grab the center pole, and adjust the bar so that one arm of the crossbar fits just under the buttocks of each skier. Ideally, the T-bar will gently pull you uphill (if you remember to keep your skis parallel and your weight centered over your feet), until, at the top, one partner pulls down on the bar and gently releases it upwards and you both ski away. In less than ideal situations (e.g., two novices riding a T-bar together and one accidentally standing on the other's skis), you will find yourself in an undignified heap a few feet from the loading area. If you've chosen a very good-looking partner (one of the major benefits of skiing single is the opportunity to meet people on lifts), enjoy the experience. If not, try to keep your sense of humor.

Enclosed Lifts

Gondolas (usually four-person) and aerial trams (holding approximately sixty people) both are enclosed lifts. You take your skis off and walk into these lifts. Your skis ride up outside most gondolas while you sit inside, whereas you stand in trams carrying your own skis. For very cold or wet weather, you will appreciate enclosed lifts—though gondolas are often slower than chair lifts and trams are frequently more expensive.

Large trams, if they don't have lines, are often the fastest way uphill. For example, the tram at Snowbird (actually two trams—with the red going up as the blue goes down and vice versa) takes under ten minutes to traverse nearly three thousand vertical feet. If you ski down (approximately two to three miles) in under ten minutes, on an uncrowded day you can catch the same tram again, ride back up, race it down again, and continue until the tram closes or your legs are totally exhausted. Local advanced skiers cover huge amounts of vertical "racing the tram."

There are two strategies to tram riding—the sane and the aggressive. The sane approach is to get in early, stand in the back, get out late, and ski down at your leisure. Aggressive skiers hold back in order to be the last skiers in and first out, then literally run through the doors to the snow, throw their skis down, jump into their bindings, and race downhill away from the crowd. If you're in the first wave out of the tram at a hard-core area like Jackson Hole or Snowbird, move fast or prepare to get trampled.

Chair Lifts

The most common form of uphill transport at most ski areas is the chair lift. They're normally called "doubles," "triples," or "quads" depending on the number of skiers they're designed to carry. Each "chair" is essentially a metal bench hanging down from a very long metal cable stretched for several hundred or thousand yards up the hill supported by tall metal pylons ("lift towers").

To get on a chair lift, you wait a few feet away from the path of the lift (the specific place is usually marked with a sign saying something like "WAIT HERE"). Just after the previous chair has passed (the lift attendant will signal you if you appear uncertain) you slide out into the path of the lift and place your boots over plastic markers in the snow (again, the lift attendant will help if needed). Look back over your shoulder, and when the lift is just about to touch the backs of your legs, sit down. As you sit, tilt the tips of your skis slightly up so they won't catch the snow as the lift moves.

Some chairs are equipped with wind/weather shields or footrests. When the chair has passed the loading ramp and is a few feet above the ground, consult your fellow riders, and if they agree, reach up and pull down on a horizontal metal bar overhead if you want to use these amenities.

While on chair lifts, try not to move around too much or swing your legs—this can cause the entire cable to sway, making riders several chairs forward and back quite uncomfortable. Also, dipping snuff and spitting or dropping litter on the skier below is generally unacceptable. At resorts with a fairly young ski population (e.g., Colorado's Front Range during Spring Break) yelling wipeout ratings at the skiers crashing below you is a popular sport. The standard scale is one to ten—with anything involving big air, multiple somersaults, and over a hundred-yard spread on detached equipment rating at least a nine.

As you approach the top ("unloading point") of the lift you'll see signs reminding you to keep the tips of your skis tilted slightly up. Move your poles to your outside hand. As your skis contact the level part of the ramp, lean forward slightly, and as the tips of your skis reach the place where the ramp begins to slope down, stand up. Make sure to keep leaning forward—most falls while unloading from chair lifts are caused by people sitting back. Let gravity pull you down the ramp—and immediately move out of the way of the next group of skiers. Even if you do fall, try to roll, crawl, or slide out of the path of the next skiers getting off the chair in order to prevent a pileup.

Although you usually decide which lift to ride on the basis of which part of the mountain you want to ski, a few other factors are sometimes worth taking into account. One is lift lines. The lifts leading directly up from the base area to the rest of the mountain are often crowded in the morning and uncrowded the rest of the day. Lifts near mid-mountain restaurants are often bottlenecks during lunch. Certain lifts are in less obvious locations than others and never develop crowds (for example, at Park City, you could often ski right on to the Crescent lift even when there were fifteen- or twenty-minute lines on Prospector). Ask lift attendants, mountain hosts or hostesses, or local skiers about where to go to avoid lines.

Another factor affecting your choice of lift is weather. Enclosed lifts (trams, gondolas, or chairs with plastic weather shields) are the uphill transport of choice in extreme weather conditions (rain, wet snow, or temperatures under ten or fifteen degrees).

New chair lift technology also is worth taking into consideration. A relatively recent innovation is the "detachable quad." These four-person chairs are like gondola cars in that instead of being fixed on the cable they attach and release themselves. This means that they move slowly for ease of loading and unloading, and then latch onto a faster moving cable to transport skiers uphill. When skiing detachable quads you spend more time skiing and less riding chairs than with traditional lifts. One potential problem with this is that unless you're in very good shape, you may find yourself getting tired early in the day. (Save money in this case by purchasing half-day rather than full-day passes).

Tips for Skiers with Bad Knees: If you have chronic knee problems, you may find that the weight of boots and skis hanging down as you ride chair lifts makes your knees hurt. To avoid this problem try detachable quads (faster uphill transport), trams, gondolas, or chairs with foot rests. (Deer Valley and Snowbird, Utah, both provide foot rests on several chairs).

Helicopters and Snow-cats (for Experts Only)

The most luxurious forms of uphill transport are helicopters and snow-cats (large vehicles that move across the snow on treads like tanks or farm machinery). For advanced skiers, these provide access to guided backcountry skiing on pristine snow. Most resorts will help you make arrangements with helicopter/snow-cat operators—or you can find information in various ski magazines.

4. SKI SCHOOLS AND LESSONS

The best way to learn to ski is to take lessons from professional instructors who have years of experience in initiating new skiers into the sport. In the United States, a national organization, the Professional Ski Instructors of America (PSIA) certifies ski instructors and insures a uniform teaching methodology in resorts across the country.

No matter how good a skier, unless your spouse or girlfriend or boyfriend or friend or "significant other" happens to be a professional ski instructor, you are unlikely to get good instruction. Very few skiers remember how difficult the "bunny hill" appears to most beginners. (A friend I tried to teach panicked on the "hill" at the edge of a sandtrap at White Pine golf course!). Moreover, teaching beginners safely is a skill.

Often lessons can help the intermediate progress from groomed terrain to bumps, powder, steeps, and other types of terrain. Advanced skiers can work on specific problem areas—race technique, deep powder, crud, trees, glare ice, bumps, crust, narrow chutes, etc. Powder lessons are the most common request at many local ski schools with bumps and racing following close behind.

Types of Lessons

Just as ski areas sell many different types of lift ticket, so ski schools offer many different lesson packages. Some common varieties follow.

All-Day Group Lesson: Consists of two hours in the morning and two in the afternoon with the same instructor. Most beginning and intermediate skiers will make substantial progress in a single all-day lesson.

Half-Day Group Lesson: A two-hour lesson that will be of most help to skiers focussing on specific problems such as unfamiliar snow conditions (moguls, powder, ice) or specific technical problems (independent leg action, skating, finishing turns).

Private Lesson: While group lessons usually have three to twelve students for each instructor, private lessons have one- to-one ratios. They're very expensive but can be useful for shy skiers or those working on things not covered in group lessons. Skiers with special needs (blind, deaf, etc.) will usually benefit from private lessons.

Beginner Package: Usually includes rental equipment, lift pass, and lesson. This is an excellent way to save money.

Ski Weekends or Weeks: Many destination resorts offer packages consisting of three or five days' accommodations, food, lift tickets and ski lessons—at substantial discounts from what these things would cost if purchased individually. If you want to move from absolute novice to intermediate skier as quickly as possible, a five-day "learn-to-ski" week is probably the most efficient way to do it.

Race Camps: Once just for racers, now race camps are opportunities for advanced skiers to improve their overall ski skills by practicing on racecourses. Many resorts offer race and other advanced clinics (usually three- to five-day packages).

Getting Ready for Your Lesson

Always plan on arriving at the ski area at least one full hour before your lesson is scheduled. (*Don't* try to "make up time" by driving fast up a narrow mountain road in a blizzard—it doesn't work.) Go to the ticket window at the ski area to buy your lift pass. Ask where to buy your lesson ticket. Some areas sell lift and lesson tickets at the same window; some do not. Ask where and when your class will meet, and try to get there on time. Wear a watch.

If some friends are escorting you to your first lesson, they may offer to take you up for a first run before your class. They will try to find some easy terrain for you. Unfortunately, most friends do not really remember the difference between an expert's idea of easy terrain and a beginner's idea of easy terrain. Having a friend help you on your first day skiing usually ruins both a good friendship and a good skiing experience. Wait for your instructor. Professional instructors know what works for beginners. Besides, they are being paid to be patient and good-natured while you make an idiot of yourself.

Group Lessons

Students who have never skied before—known in the trade as "never-evers"—are immediately assigned instructors. The instructors will start by checking your equipment, showing you how to get in and out of bindings, teaching you how to fall down and get back up, and then get you moving around on the snow.

Students who have skied previously are requested to assemble at a "splitting" area. All the students gather in a large mass approximately halfway down a green (beginning) run. One or two instructors stand with the students. Several instructors stand at the bottom of the run, usually carrying signs with the letters "A," "B," "C," "D," "E," and "F" (this is school!). A single instructor, usually a supervisor, stands halfway down the hill and signals the students to ski down one at a time.

This is without doubt the most embarrassing part of a group ski lesson. You ski toward the supervisor and are assigned to a class based on your skiing ability. (NOTE: "A" is for new skiers, "F" for advanced skiers.) A special place is reserved for the student who bounces off the supervisor then wipes out all the sign-carrying instructors like a row of dominos. Go for it.

Groups of three to ten students of similar abilities and interests are assigned to each instructor. After brief introductions, the group heads onto the hill for the lesson.

Novice Lessons

The instant you put on skis for the first time you worry about falling. Your ski instructor will teach you how to fall and get back up safely before you start skiing. She will also inspect your equipment and make sure you know how to get in and out of your skis.

After a few minutes of learning how to maneuver on flat ground in skis, you will learn how to let your skis slide downhill. You will ski slowly, with the tips of your skis close together and the tails widely separated, in a position called the "wedge." You will use a big wedge to slow down or stop, and a smaller wedge to glide downhill.

After you have learned how to control your speed, you learn how to change direction by a combination of twisting your feet and pressuring one ski more than the other. By the end of a two-hour lesson, you will be able to ski down a gentle slope in control.

If you are in a multiday program, you will gradually add new skills over several lessons. Novices use both legs in a wedge to control speed as they head down the hill. By your second day skiing, you still use the wedge position, but you learn to use your legs more independently to make turns to control speed. Your skis begin to leave S-shaped tracks down the slope.

As you progress beyond the wedge to linking turns with your skis parallel to one another, the mountain opens up for you. You find you can ski all the chair lifts instead of just the "bunny" hill. You look for enjoyment rather than survival. By the end of a five-day lesson program, you are an intermediate skier; you enjoy skiing all the groomed green (beginner) and blue (intermediate) runs while relaxing and looking at the scenery.

Intermediate Lessons

While novices are the most numerous students in single-day lessons, the most common skill level at ski week programs is "intermediate." Technically, an intermediate uses some mixture of stem christie and wide track parallel turns, with skidding more common than carving, and legs tending to work together rather than independently. From a less technical point of view, the intermediate skier is comfortable skiing most groomed runs at moderate speeds, and gets into trouble with fast skiing, moguls, ice, powder, and steep or tricky terrain.

As an intermediate, you're usually comfortable on skis and enjoy the sport, but want to ski more of the mountain, keep up with your friends, or handle varying snow conditions.

Intermediate lessons work both holistically and on isolated techniques. If you watch skiers from a chair lift, you'll notice that experts keep their upper bodies very quiet, even while skiing fast through the bumps, while intermediates often twist their upper bodies uphill at the end of a turn. In a lesson, you might work on a specific technique of planting your poles further downhill to quiet your upper body, or you might be asked to imagine Robert Redford taking his shirt off at the bottom of the run.

The main purpose of lessons at this level is to get out of the "terminal intermediate" rut—developing habits that enable you to survive difficult situations but which prevent you from mastering them—and into techniques that form the basis of advanced skiing. You will grow out of your old secure habits like you grew out of the training wheels on your bicycle—and move to new levels of confidence and competency.

Advanced Lessons

Tout piste, tout niege is a French term meaning "all slopes, all snow" and is synonymous with expert skiing. At this level you take lessons to make the transition from a good skier to an expert. You want to be able to ski notorious extreme runs with style, link turns through breakable crust, learn to race, do tricks in the bumps, or carve smoothly on death cookies.

At this level you won't see the dramatic changes that occur at the lower levels; it's mainly a matter of fine-tuning existing skills. Lessons focus more on technical details—timing of pole plant, turn initiation, line through the gates—than on broader aspects. All the basic skills are in place; you are searching for those elusive adjustments that separate your skiing from that of a World Cup racer or a competitive freestyle. Specialized race or mogul clinics will extend your range of skiing abilities.

Tips for Experienced Skiers: Dress more warmly than usual for your ski lesson. You should be prepared to spend time standing still while the instructor demonstrates techniques and helps other students. You will do far less skiing in a class than you do in a normal skiing day.

Try to get in a few runs before your lesson to loosen up. Relax. Remember, ski instructors don't spend all of their free time talking about their students' dumb mistakes—they sometimes talk about their supervisors' dumb policies.

If you want to enjoy a private or semi-private lesson for the price of a group lesson, take advantage of the worst weather you can find. During major cold snaps (weather under ten degrees) or snow storms, so few people take lessons that you're likely to be the only skier of your ability level for the day (once, during a particularly intense snow storm, I enjoyed a one-hour private lesson from the director of a major ski school after paying $5 for an inexpensive promotional "Ladies Day" group lesson).

Lessons for Women Only

Many ski areas offer either single-day women's ski lessons or women's ski weekends or weeks (e.g., Telluride and Purgatory, Colorado, Squaw Valley, and Nakiska, British Columbia) which focus on improving skiing skills by providing female instructors for small groups of female skiers, and creating a noncompetitive learning environment.

The issue of all female versus coeducational ski lessons is very similar to the issue of women's colleges. Several studies show that women from women's colleges are more successful in their careers than women from coeducational institutions. Although no one has tried to measure whether alumnae of women's ski lessons are better skiers than women who have participated in coed ski lessons, many women seem to be more satisfied with the women's programs than with the standard group lessons.

Women's ski lessons follow the same basic patterns as coed lessons. The differences are role models and atmosphere. Women's bodies are different than men's. In general, women have a lower center of gravity, higher Q-angle (angle from hip to knee), more flexibility, and less upper body strength than men. Ski technique varies tremendously with body structure. Female instructors can provide models of female bodies skiing well. Although you can certainly learn by copying male instructors' movements, the anatomical similarities of a female instructor may be helpful.

The environment of women's ski lessons is generally supportive rather than competitive. You learn almost as much from other students on the chair lift as you do from your instructor. You'll trade technical tips, commiserate about your clumsiness, or encourage each other. Fellow women will understand when you say "I always cross my tips the day before my period."

Women's lessons are as important for what they won't contain as for what they will contain. While coed lessons may be populated by a variety of teenage shredheads, midlife crisis males whose wives don't understand them, and other undesirable elements, women's lessons provide a pleasant social environment where you will meet many potential skiing partners close to your own ability level.

5. YOUR FIRST LESSON

Whether you're taking a ski lesson or trying to learn on your own, the first steps in learning how to ski are similar. Before you start skiing downhill, you need to learn how to cope with moving around on snow wearing skis.

As you walk from the rental shop to the snow, you'll notice that walking in ski boots is not easy. Boot soles are stiff and flat, and the leg of the boot is tilted forward to place you in an ideal knees-bent skiing position—which is far from an ideal walking position. On flat ground, you may look and sound like a drunken Yeti, but you're unlikely to damage yourself. Stairs and hills are a different matter.

For carrying, place the skis base to base (both shovels pointing the same way) with the ski brakes (metal prongs sticking out of the heel pieces of your bindings) overlapping to hold the two skis together. Put the skis over your left shoulder at a forty-five degree angle so that your shoulder is between the toe and heel piece of the bindings. (Some skiers prefer shovels in front and tails in back, and some prefer the other direction—try both and choose whichever works best for you.) Hold both poles just under the grips in your right hand.

While going up stairs is simple, going down stairs can be quite awkward. The easiest way is to sidestep. Stand facing (and holding) the right railing with your left foot nearest the stairs. Step down sideways with your left foot, then bring your right foot down to join it. Step down again with your left foot, then your right. As you get more accustomed to ski boots, you'll start alternating feet, but sidestepping is safest for new skiers, especially on icy stairs.

Sidestepping also is a good technique for walking up and down steep snow-covered grades in ski boots—something you'll find yourself doing walking from the parking lot to the base area and when retrieving gear if you fall while skiing. Another method for walking up steep snowy hills is similar to something mountaineers call front-pointing (when done with crampons). Point the toe of your right boot slightly down, and kick it into the snow about six inches above your left foot (this will leave your right heel hanging free in the air). Keeping your right knee bent, transfer your weight onto the toe of your right boot, then lift your left foot and plant the toe of your left boot in the snow about six inches above your right foot. Using your poles to help balance, continue alternating feet until you reach the top of the hill.

Putting Skis on and Taking Them Off

Carry your skis to an uncrowded flat area. Put your skis on the snow, approximately six inches apart and parallel to one other. Make sure your bindings are free of snow. Stand on one leg, using a ski pole to help your balance. Knock the snow off the boot you intend to place in your first ski—usually all you need to do is lift the boot off the ground and hit it a few times with a ski pole, but with fresh ungroomed snow you may need to cross your unweighted leg over the thigh of your other leg and use the tip of your pole to scrape the snow off your boot sole (see figure 5- 1a). Your boot sole must be free of snow for your bindings to function properly. Once your boot sole is clean, slide the toe of your boot into the toe piece (the piece closest to the ski's shovel) of your binding, and center the heel of your boot in the heel piece. Then step down hard with your heel. You should feel the heel piece of the binding clamp the sole of your boot. Lift your foot off the ground and wiggle it—the ski should remain firmly attached. If the ski falls off, try again, making sure there is no snow on boot sole or binding. Then, repeat the process with your second ski. If you can't get into your skis after a few tries, go back to the rental shop and ask for help.

Once you've managed to get into your skis, you should practice getting out of them. Look at the heel piece of one of your bindings. You'll notice a rectangular piece of plastic, three or four inches long and approximately two inches wide, that, when your boots are in the bindings, sticks up behind your heels at approximately a forty-five degree angle. Balancing most of your weight on the other ski, press down on this plastic lever with one of your poles. You'll feel your heel being pushed up out of the binding (see figure 5-1b). Lift your foot out of the toe piece, and repeat this procedure with your other ski. After you've practiced getting in and out of your skis a few times, you're ready to start moving.

Moving on Flat Terrain

The first set of skills Alpine skiers need to master are those of moving around on flat ground. You'll need to move forward (double-poling) and change direction (step turn).

Double Poling

The simplest way to move across flat terrain on skis is to push yourself with your poles. (This maneuver is identical in Alpine and Nordic skiing). Stand with your skis parallel and six to twelve inches apart, with your knees slightly bent. Grasp your poles and lift your arms forward, with your elbows slightly bent, to just above waist height. Hold your wrists so that your poles are pointing down and slightly back. Simultaneously lean slightly forward and drop your arms so that your

Figure 5-1a

Figure 5-1b

poles contact the snow just outside your boots. When you feel your poles contact the snow, push down and back on—and you'll start sliding forward. Keep leaning forward until your boots have slid past the tips of your poles, then pull your poles out of the snow and slide to a stop.

When you've become comfortable with pushing yourself forward and stopping, try continuous poling. After pushing, when you lift your poles up from the snow, immediately repeat the process. For additional speed, rock your upper body forward (some skiers think of this as letting their upper body fall on the poles) as you plant your poles in the snow and straighten up when you lift your poles out of the snow.

Once you feel comfortable moving forward, you need to learn how to change direction.

Tips for Experienced Nordic Skiers: As well as double poling you can use a modified diagonal stride for moving across the flats. The movement is closer to a shuffle than an aggressive racing kick-and-glide since Alpine skis have fixed heels and no grip zone. Try a diagonal stride, with smaller slower movements than usual.

Advanced Alpine skiers "skate" (double-V) across the flats. Nordic skiers will be pleasantly surprised to discover that the stiff plastic boots, fixed heels, and aggressive metal edges of Alpine skis actually make skating easier than on Nordic skis.

Step Turn

Step turns are used both for turning around in place and turning while moving. Practice step turns in place before you try them while moving.

Stand with both skis parallel and slightly separated and your poles a few inches outside and in front of your boots. Move your right pole approximately one foot to the right. Lift the tip of your right ski a few inches off the ground and move it six to twelve inches to the right—without moving the tail of your ski. Place your right ski on the snow, then lift up your left ski and place it on the snow parallel to your right one. Move your left pole to just in front of your left ski. Repeat the process (right pole, right ski, left ski, left pole) until you have completed a 360 degree turn. Try this move in the opposite direction (left pole, left ski, right ski, right pole).

After you've mastered a basic step turn in which the tails of your skis never leave the snow, you're ready for the faster more aggressive version. Move your right pole approximately eighteen inches to your right. Lift your entire right ski and rotate it until it's at a thirty to forty-five degree angle to the left one, then place it on the snow. Look back and make sure the tail of your right ski is not crossed over your left ski, then lift up the left ski and bring it parallel to the right one. Practice turning in both directions.

Once you can turn comfortably in both directions standing still, add motion. Double pole a few times, so you have some forward momentum, then try a step turn as you're moving. When you can do step turns in both directions on the flat while moving, you're ready to try a slight hill.

Falling

All skiers fall sometimes—but if you know how to fall properly, you won't injure anything other than your dignity. To practice falling, find a small area with a fairly steep grade (the steeper the slope, the less painful the fall).

The line down which a ball would roll if placed on the snow is called the "fall line." To practice falling, stand with your skis perpendicular to the fall line (across the hill rather than pointed downhill) and your poles held out away from the hill. Fall by holding your legs together and dropping your uphill hip into the snow.

To get up, place your skis downhill from your hips on the snow parallel to one another and perpendicular to the fall line. Make sure your skis are pointed across the slope rather than up or downhill. There are two common ways of lifting your body up from the snow:

The first way is to lean forward and place both hands on the snow uphill of your hips. Press down on your hands and lift your hips up, then straighten your torso (see figure 5-2).

To get up the second way, hold one pole in each hand and place the tips of the poles in the snow behind your shoulders and uphill of your skis. Press down on your poles, and lift your hips off the ground, then shift your weight forward and straighten up (see figure 5-3).

If after trying both these methods, you still can't get up after a fall, try removing your skis and getting up normally.

Ski bindings are designed to release in some falls to prevent injuries. If you've lost one ski in a fall, retrieve the ski. Look at the ski. The binding should be cocked—i.e., the plastic lever at the back of the heel piece pointed down and the ski brakes extended. If this is not the case, press down on the lever at the back of the heel piece to cock the binding.

Stand so that the boot with the ski still attached is downhill of your other boot and perpendicular to the fall line (across the hill). Place the unattached ski parallel to the attached one and a few inches uphill of it. Press down on the ski and slide it a few inches back and forth in the snow until it feels securely positioned. Using the pole in your downhill hand for balance, knock the snow off your uphill boot with the pole in your uphill hand, then step into the binding of the uphill ski.

If you've lost both skis in a fall, first retrieve the skis and make sure both bindings are cocked. Place one ski uphill of you where it will be out of your way. Place the other ski perpendicular to the fall line, and stand just downhill of it. Using your downhill pole for balance, clean the snow off your uphill boot with your uphill pole, and step into the ski. Proceed as described in the previous paragraph for your second ski.

Sliding down the Hill and Stopping

The most stable body position for moving downhill on skis is the "ready" position, similar to the stance used by tennis players waiting to receive the ball. Stand with your skis parallel and approximately shoulder width apart, your knees slightly bent, and your upper body relaxed. Your upper arms should be by your sides, and your elbows bent, so that your forearms are parallel to the ground. Point your poles back at a twenty or thirty degree angle so they won't drag on the ground. Try shifting your weight backwards and forwards between your heels and toes. Find a point in the middle where your weight is centered—evenly distributed on your feet. That's the position you'll use while skiing.

Figure 5-2

Figure 5-3

Find a short gradual downhill that terminates in a long flat runout. Move to the top of the hill, keeping your skis perpendicular to the fall line. Use a step turn to rotate your skis parallel to the fall line (pointing downhill), just like you did on the flats except for one thing—instead of placing your poles beside your boots as you turn, place them about a foot downhill of your boots to prevent yourself from sliding downhill before you're ready. You should end up with your skis pointed downhill and the tips of your poles planted in the snow on either side of your skis a foot or two downhill of your boots.

Make sure your skis are parallel, and that your body is in the "ready" position described above. Lift the tips of your poles from the snow, and relax your wrists, so the poles are pointed back as described earlier. You should start sliding down the hill. (If not, try a gentle double pole to help get started.) As you slide down the hill, remember to keep your body centered over your skis. If you feel unsteady, lean forward—most new skiers fall because they sit back away from the hill rather than keeping their weight centered or slightly forward.

When you reach the flat area at the end of your small slope, take off your skis, and hike back up to the top. Practice sliding down this short slope a few times. If you feel that you're going too fast, sit down (remember—uphill hip into the hill, feet together). Falling deliberately is much easier on your body than crashing accidentally.

After you've become accustomed to sliding downhill and drifting to a stop, try using a step turn to stop. It's very similar to the stationary step turn you practiced

Figure 5-4

earlier. Start sliding downhill, then step your right ski out to your right at approximately a thirty degree angle (so that the tip of the right ski is approximately a foot from the tip of the left one). Quickly, shift your weight onto your right ski, then lift your left ski and bring it parallel to the right one. Repeat this process two or three times, until your skis are either perpendicular to the fall line or pointed slightly uphill. You'll find yourself slowing to a stop almost immediately. Practice sliding down the hill and using step turns to both sides to stop. Once you can stop confidently using step turns to both sides (expect one side to be a bit better than the other), you're ready to get on a lift and head up the hill.

Many resorts have a hill designated for novice skiers (a "bunny hill"). Often, this hill is served by a rope tow or a very slow-moving chair lift. As a new skier, you want to stay in an isolated beginner area rather than skiing a short stretch of flat terrain at the bottom of an expert run. For example, at Snowbird, Utah, Chickadee is a green (beginner) run ideal for new skiers. On a trail map, the long green run, Big Emma, also looks like a good beginner area, but actually, it's not a good choice. The top of the bowl is quite steep, and sometimes mogulled, and on weekends it's populated with hordes of fast-moving experts heading down from the Big Emma, Wilbur, and Gad chutes. If you're not certain which runs at a resort are best for novices, ask the cashier from whom you buy your ticket or other accessible resort employees.

Etiquette

Before you head down your first actual ski run, you should know the traffic laws of skiing:

When entering a ski run, look for and yield to uphill (oncoming) skiers. (Think of this as similar to how you *ought* to behave when entering interstates from acceleration ramps.)

The uphill skier is responsible for avoiding the downhill skier.

When passing other skiers, especially on narrow runs, make sure there is adequate room, then inform the downhill skier of the side on which you intend to pass by calling out "ON YOUR RIGHT" or "ON YOUR LEFT." (When you hear these words from a skier above you, keep to the appropriate side of the trail).

Don't stop in the middle of a run—pull off to the side. Also, avoid stopping in spots not clearly visible to uphill skiers.

Stop below (downhill) rather than above (uphill) other skiers so that if you misjudge your speed or the snow conditions, you don't crash into anyone.

Intermediate and advanced skiers should offer to collect gear for fallen skiers or help injured skiers. Beginners should stay out of the way.

Ski in control. On narrow runs, a good rule is that your stopping distance should always be less than the distance you can see. Imagine (as is often the case) that around every bend is a tree or fallen skier. Don't let friends talk you into skiing on terrain or at speeds exceeding your ability level.

Obey signs. Check your trail map carefully before entering a run. The gentle inviting slope near the lift may steepen abruptly in a few hundred yards. (Snowbird's aptly named black diamond, Primrose Path, begins as a gentle groomed slope and rapidly evolves into a steep narrow mogul field. Skiers who ignore the clearly posted "Experts Only" signs at the entrance to Alta's High Traverse find, after a brief traverse, that they've committed themselves to High Rustler—one of the longest extremely steep runs in the country.)

6. BEGINNING TECHNIQUE

The first technique you'll use for skiing downhill is the "wedge" (a more exaggerated version of this used to be called the "snowplow"). Take two or three runs practicing the "gliding" and "braking" wedges described below. When you feel comfortable with both of these, you're ready to try "wedge turns." By the end of your first day or the beginning of your second day on Alpine skis, you are likely to be fairly comfortable with wedge turns and ready to try the "wedge christie." A good general rule for each exercise or technique described in this book is that once you can ski down a run without falling using one technique, you're ready to try the next one. So, for example, once you've skied an entire run upright using a wedge, you're ready for wedge turns on your next run.

Gliding and Braking Wedges

Find a very gentle slope. Start sliding down the hill in the "ready" position, weight centered, knees slightly bent, skis parallel and shoulder width apart, hands slightly above waist height and a bit over a foot apart, and poles pointing back. As you slide down the hill, slide the tails of your skis slightly apart, so that your skis are in an inverted "V." This position, with the tips of the skis together and the tails separated, is called a "wedge."

Glide down the hill in the wedge position. Try varying the width of your wedge. You'll notice that you move faster in a narrow ("gliding") wedge and slower in a wide ("braking") wedge.

Try moving your skis from a parallel position to a wide wedge. As you do this, you'll find that your ankles and knees tend to roll in slightly, and that your weight shifts to the inside of your feet. Exaggerate this natural tendency—you'll feel the inside edges of both skis dig into the snow, and you'll stop moving. The more you dig the inside edges of your skis into the snow, the more effectively your braking wedge will slow you down or make you stop (see figure 6-1).

On the other hand, as you bring your skis back from a braking wedge into a narrow gliding wedge or parallel, you'll notice that your weight shifts to the center of your feet, and your skis lie flat on the snow. When your skis are flat, they glide over the snow with almost no resistance.

Vary the width of your wedge to control your speed. Use a gliding wedge (skis flat on the snow) to accelerate or maintain your speed and a braking wedge to slow down or stop. Practice alternating between gliding wedges and braking wedges until you can control your speed comfortably.

There are a few points you should try to keep in mind as you practice your wedge:

Posture: Keep your knees slightly bent and your head erect. Most skiers, when they first practice wedges, tend to hunch over and sit back so that their hips stick out toward the tails of their skis—a very unstable position. (You'll notice this if, as you sit on the chair lift, you watch beginners practicing.) Have a friend check your posture as you ski and tap you on your hips with a ski pole if you start sitting back.

Hands: When you're practicing wedges, it's easy to forget about your hands, but letting your hands drop or your poles drag behind you can throw you off balance. Make sure you keep your hands up and forward as you ski.

Figure 6-1

Eyes Forward: Keeping your head lifted and your eyes forward will help your posture (and balance) and also prevent accidents—you don't want to crash into a lift tower as you stare at your ski tips.

Crossing Tips: Crossed tips are inevitable when you first start practicing wedges. If you try to keep your tips at least two or three inches apart at first, and occasionally glance down quickly (eyes only—don't tip your head) to check on them, you can minimize occurrences of the problem.

Wedge Turns

Although a braking wedge can control your speed adequately on gentle slopes, if you want to progress to slightly steeper slopes, you'll need to start making turns. Try to steer the tips of both skis around to the right (think of pointing or twisting your feet and knees). Then try turning to the left. If you have trouble getting your skis to turn, try the following:

Flatten Your Inside Ski. Make sure your inside ski (the left ski if you're turning to your left) is flat so that its edge isn't gripping the snow and keeping you from turning.

Turn Your Feet. Many new skiers will try turning every part of their body EXCEPT their skis. Leave your eyes, head, hands, and torso pointed downhill—and turn only your skis.

Weight Shift. To turn to your left, try shifting most of your weight to your outside (right) ski. Sometimes thinking of pressing down and away from the turn with your outside ski helps.

Half Wedge. Start sliding down the hill with your skis parallel. To start turning to your left, move only your right ski out into a wedge—and let the left ski gradually drift into a wedge as you start turning.

As you begin to feel in control of your wedge turns and are able to turn in both directions with some degree of confidence, start linking turns so that you're moving smoothly down the slope turning continuously in alternating directions.

Next, try to start shifting your weight as you turn, so that most of your weight is on the leg to the outside of your turn. See figure 6-2.

Wedge Christie Turns

You can think of a turn as consisting of three parts:

Beginning. You start traveling perpendicular to the fall line, and then, as you start turning, your skis begin to move closer to the fall line. At this point, you're moving relatively slowly

Middle. Your skis are pointed in the fall line, i.e., downhill. You normally accelerate through the middle of a turn.

Finish. As you complete your turn, your skis again turn perpendicular to the fall line—but facing in a direction opposite to the one they faced at the beginning of the turn. This is normally the braking phase of the turn, and you use it to control your speed.

Figure 6-2

At the beginning of each turn, start shifting your weight onto the outside ski (which is the one uphill at the start of a turn). Through the middle of a turn keep your weight on the outside ski, and then, after you finish the turn, redistribute your weight evenly between your two feet. To start a new turn, shift your weight to the new outside (or uphill) ski.

As you practice shifting your weight from ski to ski, you'll find that your inside (less weighted) ski will sometimes drift parallel to the other at the end of a turn. Try controlling this process consciously. As you come to the end of a turn, deliberately bring the inside ski parallel to the outside one. To do this, you'll need to make sure that your inside ski is flat on the snow (i.e., that its edge isn't gripping the snow) and unweighted (see figure 6-3)

Practice wedge christies, letting the inside ski drift parallel progressively earlier in the turn. When you can turn in both directions with your skis moving from a gliding wedge to a parallel position by the middle of your turn, you should be able to ski any green (beginner) run at any resort. (This should happen on either your second or third day of Alpine skiing—earlier if you have Nordic expertise and a bit later if you're not naturally athletic).

Don't restrict yourself to novice lifts any more. Explore all the green runs on the mountain, including those that allow you to ski the entire mountain top to bottom. After spending at least two or three hours skiing a variety of relatively long green runs or varying pitches, you're ready to start working on intermediate techniques.

Figure 6-3

7. INTERMEDIATE TECHNIQUE

The transition from beginning to intermediate skiing begins with refining the wedge christie turn you've already been practicing by adding "vertical motion."

At the beginning of your turn, stand tall, with your knees almost straight. As your skis move parallel to the fall line, gradually begin to bend your knees and ankles, until, by the end of your turn, you're bending your knees and ankles fairly aggressively. Then, after you've finished your turn, straighten up to begin the next turn. Make sure you're bending only your knees and ankles and not your upper body.

As you practice using vertical motion, you'll notice that your skis will feel "light" at the beginning of a turn, and that you'll gradually feel more pressure on the skis in the middle of a turn and the most at the end of a turn. You'll find that in this "light" phase at the beginning of the turn, it's very easy to steer your skis in a new direction, and you'll begin linking your turns more smoothly than you had before.

Putting it all together, your new turn will look like this:

1. At the start of the turn, you're standing tall, your skis across the fall line in a wedge position and equally weighted.
2. You shift your weight onto the outside (uphill) ski, and you begin to turn into the fall line. Your unweighted inside ski moves parallel to your outside one.
3. As your skis move through the fall line, you begin sinking down by bending your knees and ankles, pressuring the outside ski.
4. As you finish your turn, your skis are parallel, and knees and ankles bent and strongly pressuring the outside (now downhill) ski.
5. You move into the new turn by straightening up to lighten your skis, shifting your weight so it is equally balanced between both skis, and opening your skis into a gliding wedge.

As your vertical motion becomes more pronounced, you'll find that you need less of a wedge at the beginning of a turn. Try just using a half wedge (technically a "stem"), moving the outside ski to point into the new turn, shifting your weight, and immediately bringing your inside (unweighted) ski parallel to the outside one. After a few runs, you'll find that you can keep your skis parallel throughout the turn most of the time, and that you'll only revert to using the "stem" on steeper slopes. This type of turn ("wide track" or "skidded") parallel will enable you to ski easy blue (intermediate) runs. Spend a few hours practicing wide track parallel turns. Alternate between easy blue slopes (where you'll probably revert to using a "stem" to initiate your turns) and green slopes (where you'll be able to keep your skis parallel through the entire turn). When you feel comfortable with these rough parallel turns, find an uncrowded green run, where you can work on some additional skills.

Using Your Edges: Sideslip, Sidestep, Herringbone, and Skate

As you start skiing steeper blue (intermediate) runs, it becomes more difficult—and more important—to control your speed. To do this, you need to start using the edges of your skis more aggressively. One way to learn how to use your edges is to practice sideslipping, a technique that depends entirely on edge control.

Sideslipping

Stand on a moderate slope with your skis perpendicular to the fall line, parallel to each other, and shoulder width apart. Instinctively, in order to avoid sliding down the slope, you'll press the edges of your skis into the snow. Now, try to "release" your edges by tilting your ankles slightly downhill so that your skis are flat on the snow. When you do this, you'll start sliding downhill sideways. Stop by tilting your ankles into the hill (i.e., uphill) so that your edges are at an angle to the snow. Practice setting and releasing your edges gradually to adjust the speed at which you move downhill until you can slip directly downhill in a controlled manner (without moving either backward or forward more than a few inches) facing in either direction. You may need a few practice sessions to develop precise control (see figure 7-1).

The key to "survival" skiing is sideslipping—setting and releasing your edges to move downhill sideways. If you ever get lost or overestimate your skill level and end up on a run too difficult for your current level of skiing ability, a strong sideslip will enable you to get to the bottom safely. Another reason sideslipping is important is that it develops the edge control necessary for more advanced turns.

Sidestepping

While you're working on your sideslip is a good time to practice the uphill version—the "sidestep." Stand on a moderate slope with your skis parallel to each other and perpendicular to the fall line, and your poles planted in the snow just ahead and on either side of your feet. Start by re-planting your uphill pole approximately one foot farther up the hill. Next, lift your uphill ski and step it approximately six inches up hill. Make sure your uphill ski is perpendicular to the fall line and that the edge is firmly set in the snow—then shift your weight onto your uphill ski, lift your downhill ski and set it beside your uphill one. Finally, move your downhill pole to a position beside and slightly in front of your downhill

Figure 7-1

boot. Repeat this process a few times to walk uphill, and then try the same thing on your other side (see figure 7-2).

The Herringbone

Although sidestepping is a very safe way to walk uphill in skis (especially on steep slopes), it's also quite slow. On moderate slopes, many skiers prefer the herringbone. Stand facing uphill with the tails of your skis together and the tips apart and your poles planted in the snow behind you. Roll your knees and ankles very slightly inward so that your edges grip the snow. Step your right foot up four or five inches, keeping the tip of your ski splayed out, and move your pole to match it. This should place the tail of your right ski a few inches uphill of the tail of your left ski. Look to make sure they're not overlapping. Next, move your left ski, then your right again. After a little practice, you should achieve a continuouis duck-like waddle, which, although somewhat ungraceful, is quite efficient (see figure 7-3).

Skating

A more dynamic version of the herringbone called "skating" is useful for getting across flat terrain. Start out in the herringbone position, but instead of waddling gradually, try bending your left leg and dynamically push off onto your right one. Glide for a bit balanced on your right ski, then bring your left ski forward in the air until the tail of your left ski is crossed over the tail of your right ski at a point just behind your boot. Step out and forward onto your left ski, lifting up your right one. After some practice, you'll be able to skate smoothly across flat areas or gentle uphills.

Figure 7-2

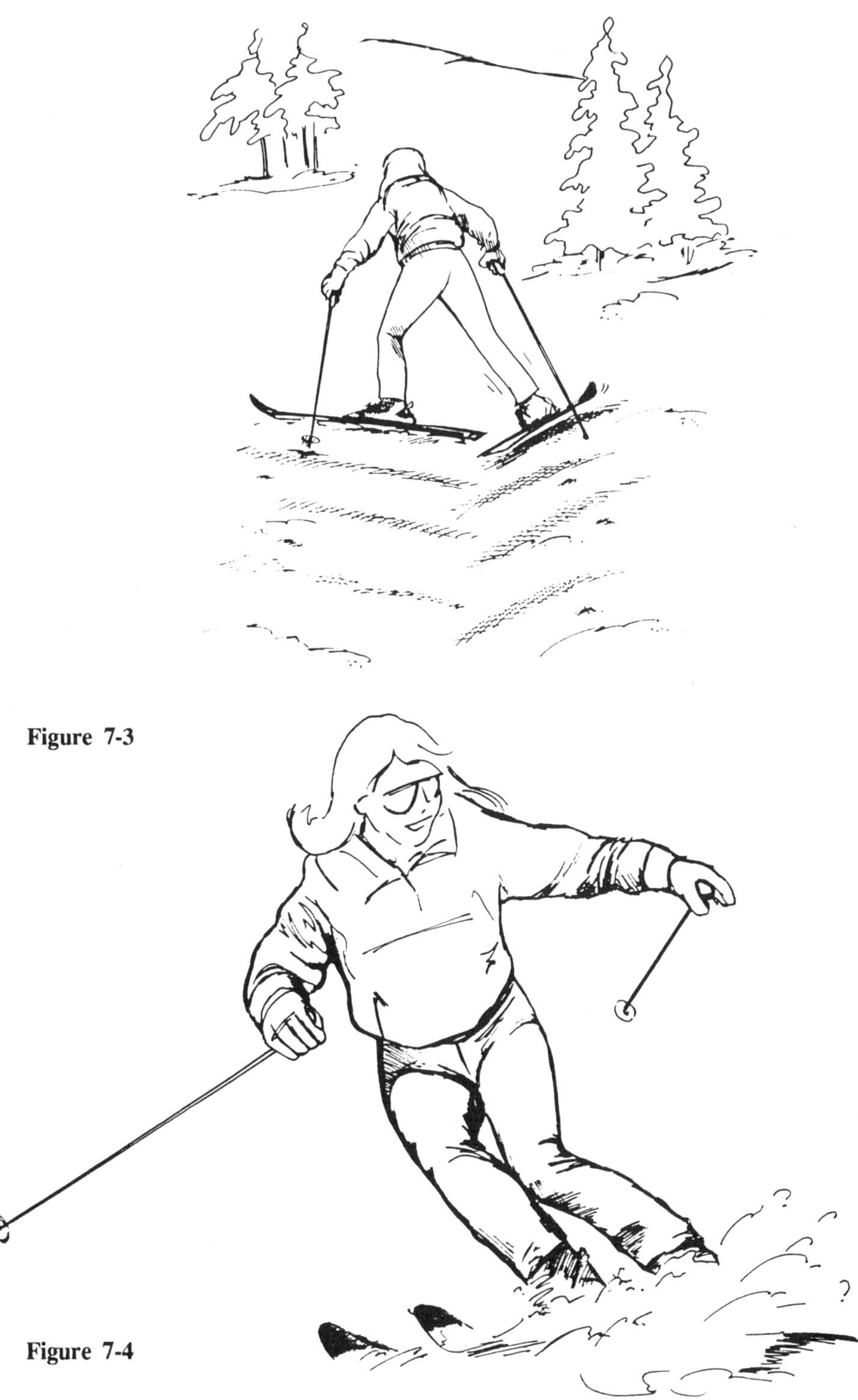

Figure 7-3

Figure 7-4

Your Edges: Stopping

A method of slowing down or stopping very popular among young skiers is the "hockey stop." Start by "schussing" (pointing your skis straight downhill) with knees slightly bent and skis parallel to pick up speed. When you are ready to stop, quickly pivot your skis so they are across (perpendicular to) the fall line, bend your knees, and dig your edges into the snow (just as you did to stop when sideslipping). You will quickly skid to a stop, dramatically spraying snow from beneath your skis. As you practice hockey stops, try to keep your upper body facing directly downhill—this aids balance and also is a good way to practice keeping your upper body "quiet" (facing downhill) while your skis change direction, a skill essential for advanced skiing (see figure 7-4).

Pole Plant

A good way to reinforce the habit of keeping your upper body quiet as you ski is to start using "pole plants." You've been holding your poles in front of you just above waist height and approximately shoulder width apart. Now, as you rise up to begin a new turn, keep both arms still. Use your wrist to move your inside pole to briefly tap the snow a few feet downhill of you.

Putting it all Together: Intermediate Turns

After practicing individual skills—vertical motion, edging, upper/lower body separation, and pole plants, try putting them all together:

Turn Initiation: After you've finished one turn, start the next:

Stand tall (lightening skis)
Plant your pole
Shift your weight toward the outside (uphill) ski
Steer your skis into the fall line
Begin to accelerate

Middle: As your skis move through the fall line:

Finish your pole plant and hold both poles a bit above waist height.
Pressure the outside ski.
Start sinking down gradually by bending your knees and ankles.
Accelerate a bit more strongly.

End: As you finish your turn:

Your skis are parallel and strongly edged.
Your knees and ankles are bent
Your upper body still faces downhill.
You are braking strongly.

This version of a wide track parallel turn will enable you to ski all blue runs and occasionally venture onto an easy groomed black. Plan to spend at least two or three ski days practicing at this level before moving on to advanced skills. This is also a good point at which to invest in a group ski lesson.

8. ADVANCED TECHNIQUE

Many skiers, especially those who ski under five days a year, find intermediate turns perfectly adequate. When you can comfortably turn on blue runs—and have a good enough sideslip or survival turn to make it down an occasional black—you can ski the majority of groomed runs at most resorts in the country, and enjoy a full day of skiing an entire mountain without wearing yourself out. If you want to try skiing steeper slopes, ungroomed snow, or racecourses, you'll need to work on advanced skiing skills; if not, now's the time to buy yourself a pair of skis and enjoy the sport.

The main difference between intermediate and advanced skiing is that while intermediates depend primarily on skidding and steering to control speed and direction, experts rely more on "carving"—setting the ski on its edge, letting the ski's sidecut cause it to turn, and using pressure to control the radius of the turn. In certain ways, advanced turns take far less strength and energy than intermediate turns—but they do require more subtlety and coordination.

The Carved Parallel Turn

Many of the elements of the "carved" parallel turn are already present in your "wide track" parallel turn—vertical motion, quiet upper body, independent leg action, and pole plant (see figure 8-1). To execute a carved turn:

Turn Initiation

Rather than steering your skis into the turn, you perform several actions almost simultaneously:

Rise up so your skis are flat on the snow and light.

Plant your pole.

Initiate your turn by slightly advancing your outside hip (moving your outside ski tip a few inches in front of your inside one) and shifting your

Figure 8-1

weight almost imperceptibly to the inside of the turn, so that your hips are actually inside (downhill) of your skis.

Roll your ankles so that your weight is entirely on the inside edge of your outside ski.

Middle

During this part of the turn you should experience the following:

You're accelerating strongly.

Your upper body is erect and faces downhill.

Your hips are shifted to the inside of the turn (amount depending on speed and shape of the turn) resulting in an angulated stance.

Your weight is entirely on the inside edge of your strongly pressured outside ski, which is bent into an arc (technically "reverse camber").

End

While "wide track" or "skidded" parallel turns end with a version of a hockey stop in which you brake by "skidding" your edges down the hill, you finish a carved turn by sinking down and strongly pressuring your outside ski. If you need to control your speed, instead of skidding, you vary the shape of the turn—finishing with a "hook" or "J" in which you maintain the pressure on your outside ski until it's pointed slightly uphill before moving into your new turn.

Rebound

When you release the pressure on your outside ski at the end of a carved turn, the stored energy will cause the ski to rebound—straighten itself out quickly and energetically. You can use this energy to dynamically propel yourself into the next turn. On steep slopes or racecourses, you may want to "skate" into your next turn, by stepping up directly onto the inside edge of your uphill ski (using the "rebound" for momentum) rather than doing a more gradual turn initiation.

Terrain and Snow Conditions

Once you can carve turns reliably on groomed runs, you have the skills to explore the entire mountain. You can start skiing steeper terrain and varying snow conditions—moguls, powder, crud, and ice. Although experts have a large repertoire of techniques for every type of snow and terrain, as a skier new to advanced terrain, you'll need a few basic "survival" techniques to handle your first encounters with new challenges:

Moguls

Practice skiing small, widely spaced moguls on moderate slopes before tackling bigger, steeper bumps. The least demanding way to ski bumps is to use aggressive hockey stops on the flat top of each bump, reach far downhill with a pole plant, quickly turn down the side of the bump you're standing on, then check on the top of the next bump.

Ice

Sharp edges are a necessity. Stay on moderate slopes, and ski delicately. Skidding (e.g., hockey stops) won't work at all. Concentrate on using the inside edge of your outside ski and finishing your turn with an uphill hook.

Powder

You can ski shallow (four to six inches) powder over a firm base using your regular carved turn. Bottomless powder (over six inches) requires some modifications:

Keep both feet fairly close together and equally weighted.

Stay close to the fall line (head almost straight downhill rather than making wide turns).

Do everything in slow motion, letting the skis come around gradually in a turn rather than trying to force them across the fall line quickly.

Shift your hips strongly to the inside of the turn to control direction.

As you finish a turn, wait until your skis plane up through the snow and become light before trying to move into the next turn.

Crud and Crust

Deep heavy snow (crud) or a thin frozen layer of ice over loose heavy snow (crust) are best avoided, but if you do get stuck in them, there are a few ways to manage it:

A straight downhill wedge is tiring and undignified, but if you need to get down a steep run covered with snow so thick and heavy that you can't turn, sometimes a wedge (no turns) will work quite well.

Exaggerated vertical motion: sink very far down into your turn, then at the end, stand up very tall, and drop your hips slowly to the inside of the new turn.

Hop turns: As you finish your turn, either jump into the air or pull your knees up toward your chest to get your skis free of the snow, and then place them back down on the snow heading in the direction of your new turn.

Racing

One of the most exhilarating sensations in skiing is the thrill of pure speed. However, just going out and seeing how fast you can go on unfamiliar terrain filled with unpredictable skiers is quite dangerous. If you want to experience fast skiing under safe controlled circumstances, the place to go is a racecourse. Most ski areas have inexpensive coin-operated or NASTAR (citizen racing) courses, and race lessons or clinics. Racing not only provides excitement but also results in dramatic improvements in your "free" (non-race) skiing skills.

APPENDIX: BUYING AND MAINTAINING YOUR GEAR

Alpine skiing is a gear-intensive sport, but if you shop carefully and maintain your equipment well, you'll be able to minimize expenses.

Buying Ski Gear

Skis are like cars—they lose nearly half their value the instant you have purchased them. A pair of skis and bindings that sell new for over $600 are available used, in perfect condition, for under $200, if you can find them.

For the best deals on new ski equipment, shop in late spring when stores are selling off everything to make room for next year's models. Pre-season (August) sales also are often worth investigating. To find used ski gear, search classified ads, buy demos from ski shops at the end of the season, or go to "ski swaps," events held in most resort towns and cities near ski areas usually in early fall.

At the end of each season, rental shops sell "demo" gear—high-performance skis they rent to prospective buyers. Since rental costs are usually applied to the cost of any skis you purchase from the rental shop, trying demo skis and buying a pair you like is a good way of both saving money and making sure you get skis that work well for you. Classified ads, garage sales, and pawn shops in ski towns are often a source of extremely cheap skis—for experienced ski buyers. Ski swaps (look in newspapers and ski magazines to find if any are held near you) are the best source of inexpensive gear.

If you're shopping for used ski equipment, you'll find the best deals by searching for basically good gear with superficial defects. The problem is separating the superficial from the serious defects.

Skis

When buying used skis, go through the following checklist:

Tops: These are 90 percent cosmetic. If gouges go through to the core, don't buy them. Otherwise, cosmetic damage improves prices.

Bindings: Look at the DIN range on the bindings. You should be at the center of the range; bindings don't perform as well at extreme settings.

Mounting holes: Each set of holes for mounting bindings weakens the ski. Especially if you are a heavy or aggressive skier, don't buy skis with more than one set of mounting holes.

Bases: Any gouges, filled or not, that go completely through the P-tex (plastic) base to the core of the ski, are very difficult to repair, and most repairs will fail under stress. Smaller scratches are easily repaired.

Edges: Look for fairly smooth edges. You can't repair edges; you replace them (not worth it) or file the edges until the bad section is removed. To get rid of a deep gouge, you might need to file off the entire edge. Also watch out for bad rust spots. If the rust goes too deep to be removed with a fingernail, don't buy the ski.

Boots

Try on boots for at least thirty minutes. Ignore missing or worn buckles and bails; they can be replaced cheaply. On Alpine boots, look very carefully at the heels and toes. If the plastic is noticeably worn, your bindings cannot function correctly. If the plastic "shell" (outside part) of the boot is in good shape and the soft inner "liner" is worn, be aware that replacing liners is fairly easy and inexpensive.

Bindings

If the skis you're buying are equipped with recent-model bindings, take them. Fairly recent used bindings are rare. Older (over five or six years) bindings are questionable. Bad antifriction plates (small white rectangular pieces) can be replaced for under $5. Since it's almost impossible to check the performance of unmounted bindings, don't risk it—saving $100 on bindings might result in $10,000 of knee surgery. Instead, look for spring sales on last year's unsold bindings.

Accessories and Clothing

Poles, goggles, and gloves are easy to buy—just search for visible defects. Check craftsmanship on gloves carefully; bad seams will leak. If you're really low on cash, buy cheap gloves and repair them with duct tape.

Check clothing for tears and bad fasteners. Don't buy anything you can't repair. If you don't mind odd colors or eccentric styles, you will do well.

Just for Women: Most women can wear boys' sizes. In fact, a size seven or nine woman is roughly the same size as a young male teenager in the middle of a growth spurt. Boy's boots and clothing cost up to 50 percent less than identical "women's" items.

Maintaining Gear

How long your ski gear lasts depends on how well you maintain it. The first step in maintaining your ski gear is deciding which pieces of equipment are worth keeping.

Skis: Everyone needs one pair of rock skis for early season thrashing. It's time to retire your old rockers and demote your current skis if:

The skis are beginning to delaminate.
Gouges go through the P-tex to the core of the ski.
Edges are so worn they can't be tuned.
Cracked edges are out of alignment.
Skis feel dead and floppy (core is breaking down).
Your skiing style or ability has changed dramatically.

Bindings: Obsolete bindings (over five years old) should be retired. Have a ski shop technician check newer bindings for wear.

Boots: Heels and toes too badly worn to mate correctly with bindings can be dangerous.

Gloves: If the insulation has worn down to the point of ineffectiveness, retire them to backup status—or use them for tuning skis.

Goggles: Replace if foam is torn or seals blown.

Clothing: Some people retire clothing the instant it becomes unfashionable but many wait until it self-destructs. If rain gear can't be revitalized with water-repellant spray and seam-sealer, demote it to windbreaker status.

The end of each ski season is a good time to sort through and overhaul all your equipment—and prepare it for summer storage.

To prepare ski clothes for summer storage, first mend rips and tears. Next, clean all garments according to manufacturers' suggestions; over long periods accumulated dirt and grunge can weaken fabrics. Rub zippers with candle wax, silicone, or other appropriate lubricant. Spray outerwear with Scotchguard or a similar moisture repellant, and treat all seams with seam-sealer (available at most outdoor retail stores). Hang garments or fold them neatly. Store wool items with blocks of cedar or moth balls.

Clean and dry downhill boots. Replace worn bails and buckles. Check for wear on removable toe and heel pieces and replace them if necessary—worn boots won't mate well with bindings. If detachable inner boots have compressed to the point where your shins get bruised, they can be replaced for a fraction of the cost of complete new boots.

Gloves also need cleaning. Use warm soapy water for cloth parts and saddle soap for leather. Treat leather surfaces with leather conditioner and cloth surfaces with water-repellant spray. Duct tape is good for temporary glove repair. Sew torn seams and treat with seam-sealer (fabric) or leather conditioner.

For goggles or glasses, investigate the possibility of replacing badly scratched lenses. If moisture has seeped into double lenses, trash them. Used fog clothes, even tightly sealed in their original plastic bags, usually dry out too much to be reusable. Use sunscreen and lip treatment over the summer—they have limited storage lives.

Car ski racks or ski attachments to multisport racks also need pre-storage treatment. Use abrasive scrubber and warm soapy water to completely remove accumulated road grime, dry thoroughly, and spray all movable parts with WD-40 or similar penetrating oil. Disassemble all components (screws, locks, etc.) so everything gets oiled.

The highest maintenance item of ski equipment are skis themselves—but tuning skis can dramatically enhance their performance and life span.

Ski Tuning

Ski tuning is a messy process. Select part of your unfinished basement for a workshop or buy a linoleum remnant to protect the floor of your work area. Next, you'll need a workbench.

The waist-high workbenches sold at most home improvement centers work well—if you have enough free space. The best alternative is an ironing board. Buy a spare cover for ski tuning. You don't want ski wax on your clothes.

Portable ski vises (sold at ski shops) attach to your workbench (or ironing board) and hold a ski steady while you work on it.

Base Repair

Place a ski in a ski vise. For some binding models (all Look turntables, for example), you can slide a screwdriver under the ski brakes to hold them out of your way. For other bindings, use a rubber strap.

Clean skis with water and paper towels. Remove remaining wax with a plastic scraper (sold at ski shops). Pour chemical wax remover over the base of the ski. Wait thirty seconds, then wipe the ski dry with paper towels. If necessary, buff the ski base with a cleansing pad (such as Scotch Brite) and repeat wax removal to insure that the base is perfectly clean.

Check the bottom of your skis for gouges. If the damage goes all the way through to the core (a different colored material), you'll need professional help. If not, light a regular candle and use it to ignite a P-tex (plastic) candle. Let the P-tex candle burn until the flame is steady and no specks of black carbon appear in the melted P-tex dripping from the lit end.

Hold the P-tex candle over the damaged area of your ski and let the burning P-tex flow into the gouge until it is filled. While the P-tex cools and hardens on one ski, work on the next ski.

When the P-tex is cool, remove any excess with a metal scraper.

Edge Sharpening

You need sharp edges to control your skis on ice. For edge sharpening, use an eight-inch mill bastard file (available at hardware or ski shops).

Place a ski in the vise with the base pointing up. Place the file flat near the tip of the ski, angled forty-five degrees to the ski's length. Hold both ends of the file. Apply enough pressure to grab the edges, but don't press down hard enough to bend the file. (If the file bends, you'll bevel the edges and they won't hold as well.)

Using short (six- to ten-inch) strokes, file the length of the ski, stopping every five or six strokes to clean the file with your wire brush.

Once you've filed the base side of the edges, rotate the ski ninety degrees in the vise so one side is up. File the side of the edge, and then rotate the ski 180 degrees and do the other side.

Clean metal shavings from the ski with a damp towel.

Base Structuring

Remember the last time you skied in wet, heavy spring snow? The suction between the wet snow and your skis made moving difficult and turning impossible. The solution is base structuring—texturing the bottom of your skis to break up the surface tension of the water under your skis.

For wet snow use 80-grit sandpaper; for average packed snow or artificial snow use 100-grit sandpaper; for dry cold powder snow use 150-grit.

Wrap the appropriate sandpaper around a sanding block and sand the entire base of the ski moving the sandpaper from tip to tail. Use the wire brush to clean the sandpaper occasionally.

After sanding the ski, rub lengthwise with a Scotch Brite pad to remove any "whiskers" of P-tex.

Hot Waxing

Ski bases should never be exposed to air, sunlight, or snow. They are made of a special plastic called "P-tex" that oxidizes, dries out, and crumbles when exposed to these elements. P-tex is designed to hold wax, and the wax is designed to slide over the snow. A waxed base not only performs better than an unwaxed one, but it lasts longer.

Ski waxes come in two types: all-temperature and temperature-specific. The all-temperature or universal waxes work well from 5 to 35 degrees Fahrenheit. Temperature-specific waxes have a narrower range but slightly better performance. If you don't race, a universal wax and a spring (red or yellow) high-temperature wax are all you need.

Wipe on waxes like Maxi-glide will help ski performance, but they don't protect your ski bases and don't last as long as hot waxes.

Start by setting your iron on "wool." Hold the wax against your iron (wear thick ski gloves to avoid burnt fingers) and let the melted wax drip on your ski—approximately one big drop every two to three inches. Adjust the iron setting so that the wax flows freely but doesn't smoke.

Iron the wax—moving the iron constantly—until the ski is evenly coated. Let the wax cool until opaque, then iron again until the wax is transparent.

Leave the wax on the skis to protect bases and edges until you're ready to ski. (If you intend to store the skis for over a month, use enough wax to completely coat the edges) Scrape off excess with plastic scraper, and buff the ski smooth with your Scotch Brite pad. You should notice a dramatic improvement in how your skis perform.

Ski Bindings

Ski bindings should be cleaned, dried, and lubricated with silicone or WD-40. Replace scratched or damaged anti-friction devices (small white slippery plates) on Alpine bindings. When you bring your skis in for a professional tune-up (once a year), have the technician test and lubricate the bindings.

Professional Tuning

A good professional ski tuning job costs \$25 to \$40. Even the best home ski tuners get a "stone-grind" a few times a year to get bases perfectly level. Major welds (repairs of huge gouges in bases) also require specialized professional equipment.

The following maintenance schedule works well for most skiers:

Full professional tune including stone-grind: Beginning of season, and every twenty to thirty ski days thereafter or when major base welds (repairs of huge gouges) are required.

Full home tune: Every five to ten skiing days. If you ski hard icy snow, you'll need to do this more frequently.

Hot wax:: Every other skiing day.

Drying skis: Every night. If you don't dry your skis with a paper towel after skiing, you'll end up with rusted edges.

Ski Tuning Equipment Checklist

You will need the following equipment for tuning skis:

Workbench: Best is a sturdy waist-high workbench. You can build your own from an old door or desktop and lumber (4X4 legs, 2X4 crossbracing). An ironing board is a cheap alternative and stores out of the way.

Ski vises: Clamp onto bench and hold ski steady for tuning.

Old ski gloves: Protect your hands from metal tools, harsh chemicals, and hot wax and P-tex.

Screwdriver or rubber strap: Binding retention.

Mill bastard file: Sharpen edges.

Wire brush: Cleans file.

Ski wax remover: Cleans skis.

Paper towels: Cleaning skis and work area.

P-tex: Base repair. Clear easiest to use.

Metal scraper: Base repair.

Candle and matches: Heating P-tex.

Sandpaper (80, 100, 150 grit): Base structuring.

Sanding block: Use with sandpaper.

Scotch Brite pad: Polishing bases.

Iron: Hot-waxing skis.

Ski wax: All-temperature hot wax. Red and yellow waxes for spring skiing.

Plastic scraper: Removing excess wax.

Workbench, files, wire brushes, sanding equipment, Scotch Brite pads, paper towels, and silicone spray are available in most hardware and home improvement stores. Specialized ski tuning gear is available at ski specialty shops near you or mail order through Recreational Equipment Inc. (REI), a Seattle-based chain of outdoor stores.

GLOSSARY

Part of learning to ski is learning a new vocabulary of skiing terms. The short glossary below will give you a good start.

Difficulty of slopes: here is a standard difficulty rating system for ski runs.

Green circle: Easiest runs. Suitable for beginners.

Blue square: More difficult. Suitable for intermediates.

Black diamond: Most difficult. Advanced skiers only.

Fall line: The line a ball would follow rolling downhill. Skiing close to the fall line is faster (and less objectionable to fellow skiers) than "zorroing"—making big wide turns back and forth across the entire run.

Grooming: Millions of dollars of grooming machines create the smooth predictable surfaces favored by most skiers. Only after extensive training on "groomed" runs do skiers acquire the skills needed to negotiate snow in its natural state.

Moguls/bumps: Mounds in snow formed by many hundreds of skiers making turns on a slope. Looks like a tilted egg carton. Fun for advanced skiers.

Outside ski: Picture a turn as a half circle. The outside ski is the one on the outside of the turn, and the inside ski is the one on the inside of the turn. Sometimes you'll hear the terms "uphill" and "downhill" ski, but these can be a bit confusing. The outside ski is "uphill" at the beginning of the turn and "downhill" at the end of a turn. In most skiing conditions, the majority of your weight is on your outside ski throughout your turn.

Racing Terms

Gates: Long, slender poles around which racers turn. Modern racing technique involves "blocking" the gates—i.e., hitting them with your arm or shoulder at thirty or forty miles an hour to brush them out of the way. Not recommended unless you're dressed like a hockey goalie or thrive on physical pain.

Slalom: The slowest type of race, with closely spaced gates on moderate pitches. A slalom turn is a short quick turn at moderate speed. Requires very fast reflexes.

Giant slalom (GS): Closest type of race to normal skiing. Gates at comfortable distance for medium radius turn at medium speeds. (Medium speeds for World Cup racers are 35-60 mph—substantially faster than most skiers' fastest speeds.)

Super giant slalom (Super G): Widely spaced gates result in turns made at close to downhill speeds. Relatively new type of race.

Downhill: The fastest way to get to the bottom of a run is to point your skis straight downhill—"schuss"—which is basically what downhill racers do. They travel at speeds over 100 mph in the fastest sections of the course. Downhill racing skis are over 210 cm. long, only turn at speeds over 40 mph, and should not be used by recreational skiers.

Freestyle: Composed of three disciplines—ballet, moguls, and aerials. Gymnastics on skis.

NASTAR: A wide-spread citizens' recreational racing program using easy GS courses safely skiable by the average intermediate. NASTAR or similar courses are often used to improve skiing skills in lessons.

Schuss: Skiing straight downhill without turning.

Snow: Skiers have nearly as many different terms for snow as eskimos do.

Corn: Melted and refrozen snow with a texture like velvet. Spring is the time for spectacular corn snow.

Crud/wet cement/mashed potatoes: Wet, heavy, soft snow common on warm afternoons or in humid climates. Highly unpopular.

Frozen granular/death cookies: Large (up to baseball- sized) chunks created by groomers chopping up solid ice.

Ice: Ranging from white ice (marginally skiable) through blue ice (for experts only). When you fall on ice you generally keep on accelerating until you hit something—like a rock, a tree, or a bus in the parking lot.

Packed powder: Oxymoron (packed snow is not powder). Ski reports use the term to mean groomed new fairly dry snow. Good skiing.

Packed snow: Groomed old snow.

Powdered snow: Light fluffy snow—highly prized by skiers.

Snowboard: A device that looks like a surfboard with bindings used as an alternative to skis primarily by younger (under twenty-five) skiers.

Turns: Skiing is turning. The most common turns are:

Wedge/snowplow: Ski tips are together, tails are separated. Used primarily by beginners at slow speeds on gentle slopes. Terms are somewhat interchangeable.

Stem or wedge christie: Skis start in wedge position, then drift parallel to one another by the end of the turn. Transitional turn for skiers moving from beginner to intermediate skills.

Wide track or skidded parallel: Skis are parallel to one another for the duration of the turn, usually shoulder width apart. Skis skid (sideslip) at ends of turns for speed control. Intermediate turn.

Carved: The skis follow an arc determined by their design with little or no skidding. The turn radius is controlled by pressure and edging rather than twisting feet.

INDEX

Acclimatization 1-2
Accident and Emergencies 21-22
Bases (ski) 7, 60, 62-64
Bindings 8-9, 34, 60-61, 63
Boots 5-7, 33, 60-61
Clothing 6-7, 9-14, 60-61
Disabilities (skiing with) 3, 28
Driving (bad weather) 16-17
Edges (ski) 7, 54, 60
Falling 36-37
Herringbone 52
Hockey Stop 54
Ice (how to ski) 57
Lessons 27-31
Moguls (how to ski) 57
Parallel Turns 29-30, 54-57
Poles 9, 34-35, 54, 60
Powder 58 P-tex 7, 62-64
Racing 58
Resorts 15-16, 18-25
Sidestep 50-51
Sideslip 50
Skating 36, 51-52
Skis 7-8, 59-64
Step Turn 36, 39-40
Stem Christie Turn 29, 49-50
Trail Map 19-20
Tuning (skis) 62-64
Uphill Transport 22-25
Wedge 29, 43-45
Wedge Christie Turn 45-46
Women 30-31, 60